More Than Numbers:

Mathematical Thinking in the Early Years

edited by Dennie Palmer Wolf and Bonnie Neugebauer

published by Child Care Information Exchange

Dennie Palmer Wolf is a senior research associate at the Harvard Graduate School of Education. She has researched and written widely on children's symbolic development.

Bonnie Neugebauer is the editor of *Child Care Information Exchange*.

Cover Photograph: Bonnie Neugebauer

Copyright © 1996 by Child Care Information Exchange
PO Box 2890   •   Redmond, WA 98073-2890

This book is a revised and updated version of a collection of articles originally published as Beginnings magazine, Winter 1985, published and copyrighted by Exchange Press Inc. Biographical information has been updated whenever possible.

ISBN 0-942702-19-0
Printed in the United States of America

More Than Numbers:
Mathematical Thinking in the Early Years

Masculine and feminine pronoun references in this book are used randomly for simplicity and in no way reflect stereotyped concepts of children or adults.

One, Two, Three . . . A Lot: Getting a Deep Understanding of Numbers

by Marguerita Rudolph

Not infrequently, adults mistake young children's correct counting for actual knowledge of numbers and offer praise when, in reality, children are only saying words. The fact is that young children are capable of memorizing numbers in proper sequence and saying them easily, so it sounds intelligent to adults. "That's right, Mimi. You can count." And Mimi, encouraged by praise, concludes that saying it right means counting. In reality, children often confuse using numerals to name things with the process of counting.

When a dispute erupted among two four year olds over the number of blocks each needed, a teacher went over to mediate. "George, tell Paul how many blocks you need, instead of grabbing and making him mad." That seemed acceptable: the two boys followed the advice literally, without thinking. "I want ten," George said randomly to Paul. Paul did not even have ten in his supply. But he did not consider that a problem. He began to count with George, watching him approvingly. Paul counted aloud correctly, placing a finger on a separate block as he said each number, touching some blocks more than once. The block he touched when he said *ten* was the one he handed to George. Both children proceeded peacefully, each with his own building.

Clearly, there was no concept of ten on the part of either of them. In that situation Paul was saying and George was listening to words that represented counting to them. For them, counting sequentially by touching objects didn't mean that each more advanced number included the previous ones. George and Paul's teacher had assumed that counting in the correct sequence meant that children understood the meaning of counting. When she asked "How many?" the boys understood her to be asking them to go through the verbal exercise of counting. But watching the boys, she learned a lesson about what counting is to young children.

Robert, hearing his mother tell another adult, "He's four," protested: "I am not four! I'm Robert." Confusion is not uncommon when children are counted by designating each with a number. "No, I am not THREE (when the child is third in line); I am FOUR!" (meaning years of age).

When all 12 of the preschoolers were gathered in the classroom for the first time, Mrs. K. was impressed by the very presence of all of them. "Let's see how many children we have," she said, touching each child gently as she counted. The children enjoyed being counted, but she sensed that there was little comprehension of counting on their part.

As the children played, she had a vivid math lesson from one of the children. Lisa had noticed a geo board on a table with three rubber bands still stretched on it. Later when she came back to it, there were only two left. Lisa complained, "I need three rubber bands."

"How many are there?" the teacher inquired.

Lisa went over and counted thoughtfully: "One, two . . . I need three."

Her teacher handed her one more rubber band (the three Lisa had been

wanting). "How many are there now?"

Again Lisa counted slowly, a tone of delight coming into her voice when she got to three.

So, No Counting?

Does all of this mean that there should be no counting in the classroom? On the contrary, there are plenty of contexts in which counting is just the right thing to be doing. Children perform many informal investigations involving counting: stacking unit blocks to a particular height, extending them for length, determining just the right size block to use in a particular place.

However, if counting is going to be meaningful, it is important to keep several things in mind:

Make way for personal experiments. Noel, standing not far from his mother, is playing with a pile of small stones in the back yard. Picking up one stone, he takes it to a nearby bench and places it on the surface with nothing else around it. Then, after contemplating the stone, he looks at his mother and proclaims: "This is ONE!" His mother recognizes his accomplishment with a look as Noel hurries back to the pile. Noel takes another single stone, runs to the bench and, placing it near the first, he announces, "This is TWO!" With increased excitement, Noel runs again to the pile to take another single stone. He places it quite precisely near the other two stones. He exclaims with a sense of discovery: "It's THREE!"

Not wanting the triumph to come to an end, Noel rushes to his handy

Photograph by Subjects & Predicates

stone supply, picks up another single stone, and unhesitatingly places it next to the other three. "This is . . ." he begins. And here the triumph almost ends. Noel looks perplexed. He can't go beyond *three* in this situation. But since Noel is his own teacher here, he plunges ahead, to the delight of his uninterfering mother. Recognizing his own limitation, he quickly finds a way out. "This is," he says soberly, taking a deep breath, "a LOT!" (adapted from Rudolph and Cohen).

Noel may not count, but intuitively he handled a single stone at a time in an uncluttered area (teachers, take note). He found a term for each new stone, and he recognized when he came to a stopping place and could go no further. Had his mother prompted him with her word *four*, she would have prevented rare mathematical insight. Noel might have simply parroted his mother's word *four* without it having meaning for him.

Respect children's respect for their own limits. Children are very good at providing signals about when *it's enough* or *too much*. Here is a little girl with her grandfather:

Grandpa shows her one spoon. "How many is that?"

"One," she answers.

Then he shows her two. "How many is that?"

"Two," she says.

Then Grandpa shows her three spoons. "And how many is that?"

The little girl looks down disdainfully. "Take that one away — it's dirty, don't you see?"

In the words of Chukovsky, the little girl was "masking the discomfort from ignorance," and, like Noel, she

recognized her ignorance beyond two. She also tells her grandfather that she is not ready to count beyond two, especially when being quizzed by an adult. If we listen to children, it is easy to tell when and how they are ready to count and calculate.

Personal involvement. In situations where there is personal involvement, a preschooler can be amazingly mathematically accurate!

Stevie: "My mother is still in the hospital and guess what? She had a baby and the baby is not big enough to come home yet . . . this one is a brother, and I'll be a big brother to the baby. . . ."

Teacher: "So your family is bigger now."

Stevie: "We have five in the family now: my father, my mother, my big brother Jim, and me."

That was meaningful counting, proceeding from the child, with the teacher being a sympathetic listener and responder to family news — so important to a child just five years of age.

Young children will even spontaneously use fractions when they are motivated by need or have made some careful observation. My three year old neighbor Michael noticed the gradual disappearance of the chicken pox scabs from his body. "Only one chicken pox left," he told me, then added to be precise: "It's halfway off."

Permission for mistakes. There is nothing young children like better than to be a part of the real life in which they get to use kitchen knives, answer the phone, snap the camera shutter. Because of their appetites in this direction, activities like cooking provide vivid situations in which to learn about mathematics. Tasty

results are less important than working with a small group of children to create an atmosphere where children can recognize that it's possible to learn from mistakes.

In one cooking session, I wanted to acquaint children with different kinds of sugar, so I chose a recipe calling for half brown sugar and half white sugar. As soon as we sat down to taste, the children discovered that what we had baked was less than sweet. We checked the ingredients and learned what we had left out. After that, the children always remembered to check the list. Moreover, they carried the idea of checking over to other projects.

Going Beyond Counting

It is not enough for children to use numbers in the one situation of enumerating objects. They deserve a chance to use the counting series in many different ways.

Physical measuring. Many infants and toddlers are entertained by and respond to traditional finger plays, such as "This little pig went to market." In such games, even young children are involved in orderly enumeration, one important ingredient in counting. With only a little encouragement from adults, older preschoolers engage in hand and finger play involving counting, adding, and subtracting.

Such practice provides more meaning and familiarity to the act of counting than the numerals and icons in many workbook exercises. In fact, Claudia Zaslavsky, who has made a special study of finger math in children and primitive peoples, describes how this kind of physically immediate counting is coming to be recognized as the child's first *calculator* (Zaslavsky).

Equally intriguing to children is the idea of

Photograph by Francis Wardle

will also gain physically based respect for tools and instruments of measurement.

Describing. Children have to forge the connections between the different kinds of quantity words they have: such as numbers and descriptors like big and bigger. The word *big* is probably one of the most common words in a young child's vocabulary. He hears it spoken with positive stress in relation to himself. *Big* is undoubtedly good, and *bigger* is better, or worthier. "I am big" is a spontaneous proud utterance from young children. My neighbor Michael compared relative size and strength with a friend, and then asked his mother: "Is big strong?" And then later on, he asked thoughtfully, "Is 100 years very strong?"

Big is also an attribute bearing on age. To a young child, getting older means getting bigger. Thus, when a group of five year olds in an after school program visited some senior citizens who were celebrating a man's 100th birthday, they were apprehensive. Afterwards, the children expressed surprise, "Why is he so little?" "But he was so small. . . ." They had expected 100 to be giant sized.

Novel Numerical Materials

Too often children grow up applying numbers just to the number of crackers in the basket or the number of colored dots on the workbook page. But why? There are many intriguing, rewarding materials that give life, even a kind of handsomeness and elegance, to numbers.

Geometry is natural. Teaching children the three basic shapes — circle, square, and triangle — seems to be a standard in early education. But how dull the printed forms tacked up on a bulletin board must seem to children who are eager for experience. Circles, squares, and triangles abound in

measuring by arm's spread or footsteps. For example, when a child asks for twine for outdoor or dramatic play, a teacher might help out by suggesting the child measure the amount needed with arm's length. Or children

can use their own footsteps to mark out several equal areas for block-building. Children may not measure precisely — they may take longer and shorter steps. But they will understand the concept of counting off distance using a part of their body. They nature, as well as in objects made by human hands.

A bowl of fruit can teach much about transformations, geometry, and number. Cut an apple horizontally to reveal the cross-section, handing out slices to every child to hold, look at, and respond to. Inside the one circle they will find a five-pointed, star-shaped seed container with dark seeds on a white circle of apple flesh.

In the same spirit, cut an orange into thick circles, slit the peel, slowly straighten the circle so it becomes a straight line. From the one slice comes a line of many separate, perfect triangles. Or spread the all-too-familiar square pieces of sandwich bread with a filling. Make a sandwich, cut it diagonally. How many cuts did it take to make how many triangles? Do it again and again. Now how many cuts and how many pieces? What is happening to the pieces as you make more cuts?

Reading, literature, and playing. Many stories and rhymes show that counting is part of life.

Here is a wonderful Mother Goose rhyme which might touch on some of the mystery that young children feel in response to the whirl of number terms around them:

There once were two cats of Kilkenny,
Each thought there was one cat too many.
So they fought and they fit,
And they scratched and they bit,
Till, excepting their nails
And the tips of their tails,
Instead of two cats, there weren't any.

The Teacher's Role

It is more important to be an observer of children's working-thinking-doing than to be a teacher who prods and prompts.

Leeb-Lundberg uses the term *teach* in quotes:

It is very important to realize the psychological development the child is going through, so that we do not mistake some half-knowledge of the developmental process of mathematical concept formation and try to "teach" him things which he can only, in the privacy of his own mind, go through with the aid of a multitude of practical experiences.

References

Apelman, M. "The Missing Link: Reflections on Mathematical Beginnings," **Outlook**, No. 33, Autumn 1979, Mountain View Publishing Co., Boulder, Colorado 80302.

Leeb-Lundberg, K. "The Block Builder Mathematician," in **The Block Book**, Elisabeth S. Hirsch (editor), NAEYC, 1974. Third printing.

Rudolph, M., and D. Cohen. **Kindergarten and Early Schooling**. Englewood Cliffs, NJ: Prentice-Hall, 1984.

Zaslavsky, C. "It's Okay to Count on Your Fingers," **Teacher**, February 1979.

Zaslavsky, C. **Preparing Your Children for Math**. New York: Schocken Books, Inc., 1979.

Marguerita Rudolph had a wealth of experience teaching young children — and was the author of two books, ***Kindergarten and Early Schooling*** *and* ***Should the Children Know?***

A Toddler's Two

by Erin Phelps

"One, two, three," says Nora as she climbs three steps. "She's already counting?" asks my friend, climbing up behind her. I stiffen up with pride, then blush at being so proud. "Not really," I finally answer. After all, Nora's adding three onto her counting sequence was a new event.

Thinking back on that moment, I see that I was both right and wrong. On the one hand, Nora hasn't repeated her "One, two, three" since then. But in another way, I was not so right. Ever since she was 18 months, Nora has been working on understanding just what two means. It's been hard work, arduous at times, but by concentrating just on grasping the idea of *twoness*, Nora has the foundations of counting.

Usually I am not a parent who keeps detailed records of every move my daughter makes — it would take too much of the joy out of motherhood. But one day, when I shared some of Nora's number stories with Dennie Wolf, she asked if I would keep close watch on how Nora was building her understanding of numbers.

The process of watching and writing, odd as it is for me, has increased my understanding of the way children's interactions with other people affect their learning, even of such apparently fixed and formal concepts as numbers. I hope this comes through as I write about Nora learning about two.

The Very Beginning

For Nora, the beginnings of the use of numbers came out of her physical activity. As he gets ready to go down the slide with Nora, her father always counts, "One, two, three, GO!" About the age of 18 months, Nora started chiming in, "One, two, nine." In fact, these number words were among her earliest understandable sentences. Nora may have picked up these number words and the idea of stringing them together from her father and from her babysitter who does exercise routines.

But even in these earliest tries, she was not just parroting back what she had heard. (No one around her counted, "One, two, nine.") She was already interpreting what she observed other people doing. Soon, if someone said, "O-o-one, . . ." Nora would finish it off, ". . . two, nine!" and clap her hands in excitement. These routines went unchanged for several months. They are probably closer to pure language play than counting.

As Nora's language began to take the form of labeling, she came closer to counting. Instead of numbers being part of a chant in an exciting situation, Nora began to draw the connections between particular objects and number words. The earliest example took place one morning when she looked straight at the crooked top and wide base of a coat hanger and said, "Two!"

This was a startling example to me of just how differently Nora sees the world. Once she had called out "Two," I could see that the hanger looked like the numeral, but I would never have made the association myself. When I think of two, I think of pairs of objects. For Nora, at 20 months, two wasn't a quantity, it was what you call all kinds of two-shaped items. Here, too, I am sure that

Photograph by Bonnie Neugebauer

Nora's knowledge of the shape name came from images of numerals in her picture books and from what she had seen on "Sesame Street." But even though she may have simply been using a well-rehearsed label, she was interpreting and experimenting with it.

Something Like Counting

Along with this labeling behavior, Nora began to work on routines that seemed much more like counting, in the sense of taking stock of all the

items in a set. For example, when she was 23 months, Nora began to line up three Fisher Price dolls or three blocks and call them "One, two, nine" or "Mommy, Daddy, Nora." Each block or doll received a specific label as it was picked up or touched. This was different from her earlier pronouncing of "one, two, nine" with no objects in sight. Similarly, Nora often wanted to do exercises. She would lift her legs and say, "One (lift), two (lift), nine (lift)" or lift them as someone else counted out the usual sequence,

"One, two . . . ." This was the beginning of accurate use of counting words to mark objects or actions.

As her second birthday approached, we tried to teach Nora the correct answer to the question "How old are you?" We would answer "Two" for her and hold up two fingers. Soon she began to imitate these behaviors exactly. At the same time, we tried to teach her the difference between being *home* and being at our camp in *Maine*.

Unfortunately, we asked "Where are we?" with the same intonation as we asked "How old are you?" As a result, she would randomly answer either question with any one of the responses: "Maine," "Home," or "Two." So even while something quite like counting was beginning, a word like two was a word you answer questions with, rather than the name of a quantity or an amount.

The Idea of a Quantity

After her birthday, the "one, two, nine" rote list changed to "one, two, one" and has been pretty stable, with the exception of the one time when she came out with "one, two, three" on the stairs. However, the word *two* now means an amount or quantity.

One day Nora said, "Two," holding up two dolls and seemed surprised. This quickly extended to all pairs of objects — two hands, two blocks, two flowers, two forks — and was correct every time. Nora now knows one of the meanings of two in the mature sense. More importantly, she has put two objects together in relation to each other and has constructed the

abstract idea of this relation. So strong is her understanding of this relation that she can create it and label it across all kinds of objects. This is the root of the notion of quantity as a way to describe a set of objects.

At first, this proper use of two occurred only spontaneously. Whenever someone asked Nora how many things she had, she was just as likely to say "Home" as "Two." In more recent weeks, the answer is usually right. Similarly, when asked to pick up two blocks, Nora usually obliges, often adding in, "One, two." The notion of a one-to-one correspondence (one numeral for each object) and the idea of special names (like two) for sets of certain sizes are beginning to come together. This marks the extent of Nora's number development at this time. The "one, two, three" example on the stairs suggests that she is on the threshold of three, but right now such behaviors are only very scattered.

Of course, Nora's behavior is quite limited, even now. The concept of three is still missing, except in the rote sequence of "one, two, three" (and, in fact, the sequence "one, two, one" occurs more often). Higher numbers don't exist, even as labels. Nora doesn't have words for more, many, or lots. She doesn't even use the concept of one. Maybe it represents only something to which contrasts are made and which needs no label of its own.

What does all this say about number development? Right from the outset, Nora's use of numbers was social. Her "one, two, nine" sequence was social — a way for her to interact with

her father on the slide. Even her later uses of "one, two, nine" were social — they were often a part of joint language play and games. Many of her uses of two occurred in question-answer exchanges, at a time when Nora understood two to be an answer word, rather than a number word. Other uses of two took the form of labels for particular shapes — something she had observed us using to label pictures in books and "Sesame Street" characters doing on television. Similarly, Nora may pick up the idea of pairing numerals, objects, and pointing from observing adults, other children, or television characters doing the same.

Even though Nora learned about numbers through interactions with other people, what she did was never just imitation. No one around her counted, "One, two, nine." Nor did anyone hold out a hanger and call it two. Moreover, the idea of two, the concept of a pair, can't be imitated. Nora had to build her own notion of twoness before she could label pairs of dolls, socks, flowers, and forks by calling out "Two." Once I look at all the interpreting and inventing that Nora has done to get to the brink of three, I am impressed. She has a very basic notion of quantity and more will come.

Erin Phelps is a developmental psychologist who studies the growth of children's mathematical and logical thinking and assistant director for technical services at Murray Center at Radcliffe College.

Number:
Part of a Larger Logic

an interview with Constance Kamii by Dennie Palmer Wolf

When I ask someone where children get their number concepts from, most often they give me a list of nonsense. Some say children learn number by learning how to count. That's wrong. Some people say that children learn number concepts from observing and comparing sets of objects: three apples and three marbles, two bananas and two shoes, and so forth. Another explanation is that children learn number concepts from manipulating objects. And then there is a whole lot of other wishy-washy stuff like "They learn number by having experiences." That always makes me want to ask, "What kind of experiences? A birthday party? A trip to the zoo?"

So where does number come from? I need to explain the logical nature of number using a task developed by Jean Piaget, the Swiss psychologist. You give a four year old child a glass and a pile of chips and you also take a glass. You tell him, "Each time I put one in my glass, you put one in yours." You thus drop some chips into the glasses one by one. Then you say, "Let's stop. Watch what I am going to do." You put one extra chip just in your glass. Then you start again with one-to-one correspondence. You keep going until there is no way that the child can tell the difference in the number of chips in the glasses by looking at them.

After you stop, you ask: "Do we have the same amount? Do you have more or do I have more?" Many four year olds will guess,

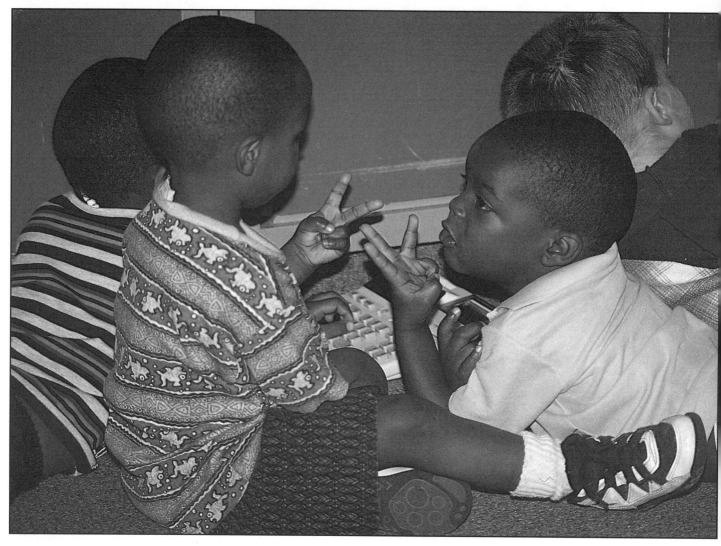

Photograph by Bonnie Neugebauer

but they don't know. You interview them and they can tell absolutely everything you did — every empirical fact; but they cannot draw a conclusion logically.

Four year olds who can count to 30 or 100 do not have the logic to answer this question with conviction. What they have is what Piaget would call the social or conventional knowledge of counting. They also have a great deal of what Piaget called physical knowledge — they know the colors of the chips and how heavy they are and that they are lighter than a quarter.

But to solve this number problem a child must have logical knowledge: If one more was put into your glass, no matter how many chips were put in one to one, there is and will always be one more in your glass. Number develops out of this kind of logic and not from counting or from observing sets.

Now immediately that should have implications for how we teach number. The best way to teach what is important for mathematics is to get children to think logically ALL the time. Let me give a real example:

A mother wanted her five year old to put out napkins for dinner for a family of four. He knew how to count to

30; but when he had to put four napkins on four plates, he made four separate trips to the cupboard. He went to the cupboard and took one napkin and put it on one plate, then went back to the cupboard and took another napkin and put it on a second plate, and so on.

Then one day I guess he thought about counting. He counted the napkins, "One, two, three, four." That was fine as a system for a few days. But then one day there was a guest, and five plates were laid out. So, as usual, the child went, "One, two, three, four." But that left him with an empty plate. He was quite puzzled; he collected all four napkins and put them back and made five separate trips. For the next few days, he stuck to that strategy.

Then he went back to counting for several days. But then there was a guest again. So he thought about the plates, counted them to five, and then counted out five napkins and distributed them. After that, according to his mother, he never went back to all those trips again. Now that is an example of getting the child to think. If the mother had said, "Count the plates, count the napkins, do this, do that," that five year old would just have been an obedient success.

The development of logic takes place all the time and is not limited to numerical thinking. Every day, there are many different ways to get children to think logically. Take the case of art class: Often teachers say, "First you color the plate, then you put the holes near the edges, then you tie the string on. That's how you make the mask." It would be much better to hold up the mask and say, "How do you think I made this? What did I have to do first? Then what did I do?" Let children figure it out.

In conflict situations, which come up all the time, teach children to think through a solution. If two children are fighting over a toy, adults very often say, "Okay, if you fight, neither of you can have it." Or they use a timer to give five minutes to one child, five minutes to the second child. That is very unthinking. It is bad for children's cognitive and moral development. A more effective way is to say, "I will keep this toy so you two can decide how you are going to solve this problem. When you decide, then come and get it." You have to get children to think and think and think, all day long. Children who can think will build number concepts earlier than those who have not been encouraged to think.

Adults have to watch out for their tendency to just tell kids how to count, how to add, how to play a game correctly. Suppose there is a squabble because one of the children turns over three, not just two, cards in a game of "Concentration." Again, it is so easy just to make the correction. I would say to children, "What do you think about that?" And if they say it is okay, it is okay. *They* decide. But then the next one will also want to turn three cards over, and that will be another point of discussion. It is the fact of arriving at an agreement, not how many cards it says in the rule book, that matters.

Or, you put out the cards, and all at once there are four or five children crowding around, saying: "I wanna be first!" "Me first." "My turn to be first." It is simplest just to pick someone. But how much better to say, "Everyone wants to be first, can you think of a way to decide?" Then children have to decide what is just and right.

Everyone thinks that they should spend their time correcting things like children saying *eleventeen*. But this kind of social knowledge is superficial. At one age a child may say, "I thinked it up in my head"; but a few months later the child is saying, "I thought it up." Counting is like that. Logic is more basic and harder to acquire than words. So logic is what we should teach.

In all of this, it is important to pay attention to what children are thinking about, not what is literally correct. Suppose some five year olds want to see whether the swings or the slide is closer to the back door. Say they decide to do it by pacing the two distances off — but in one case they take long steps and in the other case they take smaller steps. Or they take a winding route in one case and come to the wrong decision. A teacher could intervene at that moment with all kinds of ideas on how to measure correctly, how to use straight lines and equal units of measurement. But five year olds don't understand these concepts. If the teacher insists, he's missing the point.

The point is to figure out how the children are thinking. They may be comparing how long it takes to get to the swings or how hard it is to get there and using numbers to describe whatever dimension they have in mind. It's enough for them to have thought about how far into the strategy of using paces and comparing the numbers they got. Those are the kinds of thinking processes teachers should be fostering.

Now, if those children disagree, it may be time to get them to talk to one another again. Or it may be time to do something diplomatic, "Peter measures his way, you measure your way."

All of this may sound as if teachers should take a back seat. But no, their role is tremendous. Only *they* can place children in the role of decision-makers. I know it is easier to say, "You go first." I know it takes more time to ask, "How are we going to solve this?" But without teachers taking that time, children will never have the logic they need; and that is the key.

Reference

Kamii, Constance. **Number in Pre-school and Kindergarten**. Washington, DC: National Association for the Education of Young Children, 1982.

Constance Kamii is professor of early childhood education at the School of Education, University of Alabama, Birmingham. She is the author of many articles and books on children's early mathematical learning.

Beyond "1, 2, 3 . . .": Computers and Mathematical Thinking

by Douglas H. Clements

Marcie and Lynn are programming the computer to draw a submarine. They've finished the body and are halfway through the propellers. Lynn spontaneously uses the mathematical ideas of symmetry and equivalence as she suggests what they should next tell the *turtle* — a small triangle on the screen — to do. "The top is the same as the bottom. Push *F* (for Forward) three times again." The girls work around to the top and start back down. "How far?" Marcie reasons: "It's three to match the other side and then . . . umm . . . half of the middle part — that was four — would be two and three is five!" They finish the project with a periscope: "Hey! We can use the *L* from *Lynn*." "What?" "Yeah, just put it upside down." These four year olds, part of a computer research study, are engaged in sophisticated mathematical thinking involving such concepts as equality, division, addition, and rotation.

Mathematical Thinking

What exactly *is* mathematical thinking? Can — and *should* — computers be used to help young children learn mathematics in new ways? Mathematics is not just counting and naming numerals. It involves a combination of conceptual knowledge (the ability to understand things) and procedural knowledge (the ability to do things). Children should come to *understand* mathematical concepts, such as numbers and space, and how concepts are related. They should also learn to *do* mathematics by solving problems: Mathematics is also a *way of thinking*.

This seems plausible; children *should* develop high-level thinking processes. But don't they need practice for mastery? An answer to this dilemma has come from research in psychology: *There are two different types of mathematical thinking.*

One, *automatic thinking*, involves fast, effortless performance. If certain skills and facts are not learned well, too much of children's thinking (cognitive processing capacity) is used up. There is not enough left for higher level problem solving. For example, children ultimately have to be able to count forwards and backwards from any number, without having to *think about it* too much.

The other kind of thinking is *reflective thinking*. Here, children are consciously aware of the problem and the solution processes they use to solve it. While it is still true that children need lower level skills and knowledge to become *experts*, they also need to develop reflective thinking at each stage of their development of mathematical knowledge. Therefore, from the earliest years they need to be challenged to solve problems based on the skills and knowledge they currently possess. This helps them organize all their knowledge into strong, useful frameworks upon which future learning can be built.

In somewhat simplified terms, then, we actually want students to act *unconsciously* in some situations and quite consciously in others. Both types of mathematical thinking are needed to develop micromathematicians.

Enter the computer. As an all-purpose device, it is ideally suited to provide the different types of experiences necessary to develop different types of mathematical thinking. As a

highly interactive device, it is ideally suited to engage energetic young children with opportunities for active learning. However, worthwhile software must be used, and it must be used appropriately.

Computer-Assisted Instruction for Reflective Thinking

Computer-assisted instruction programs can also put children into a generative role, inventing mathematical ideas. They learn to play with (construct) ideas as they play with the programs. These programs might be games, simple simulations, or creative *construction sets*.

Integrating Computers into the Classroom

To plan for the sound integration of the many possible applications of computers into the classroom, an analogy with a tree is helpful. The branches represent different approaches to learning. Although each branch has attractive *foliage*, such as graphics, animation, and sound, the important characteristic of the branch is the type of mathematical thinking it supports, each of which is an important contributor to the overall development of the child. As on a tree, the branches are part of an organic whole — they nurture and support one another.

Like a tree, the most attractive part of educational computer programs is on the *top* or surface level — the graphics, animation, sound, and interactivity. However, if the program is not rooted in solid theory and principles of learning, it will not develop, or even stand up!

Therefore, it is important that goals and principles be considered first and then computer programs evaluated to ascertain if they support the

type of mathematical thinking desired and if they are rooted in sound principles.

Evaluation checklists can help, but it is most important to ask:

• What am I trying to accomplish? Will the program help?

• Will this program develop automatic or reflective mathematical thinking as appropriate?

• Does it do this better than I could without a computer?

Automatic Thinking

For those essential skills and facts that children need to learn very well, computer-assisted instruction (CAI) programs can provide motivative practice with immediate feedback. For example, there are more programs that provide practice on the counting and number-numeral correspondence than you can count. However, achieving a level of automatic thinking in counting is not a simple task. It is easy for children to harbor misunderstandings about it.

One of my kindergartners, when asked to count, stood straight up and counted to ten. Praised and asked to count backwards, he *turned around* and counted "one, two, three. . . !" Because such misunderstandings exist, programs should be mathematically and developmentally sound.

1. Drill should be used immediately after an understanding of the concepts has been developed.

2. Children should have the intent to memorize and respond automatically (quickly).

3. Use short, frequent sessions in conjunction with regular conceptual review.

4. Introduce only a few new facts/skills at a time.

5. Vary drill activities and ensure enthusiasm remains high.

6. Praise children and keep visible records (e.g., simple charts). Better computer programs store records. Make sure children develop a strong self-concept as they develop skills.

7. Make sure children practice only those skills on which they need practice. Better programs automatically assign children to that material they need to learn.

8. Practice those skills which require immediate feedback (e.g., counting or instant recognition of small numbers).

Reflective Thinking

1. Know exactly what your goals are in using the program.

2. Establish *class experts* who can help others.

3. To help the whole child develop, encourage children to play games together. Make the experience a positive one socially and emotionally, as well as intellectually.

4. Teach for *transfer*, so that children will be able to apply the knowledge they learned on the computer to off-computer situations:

• Make sure concepts are well learned.

• Talk it out — through questioning and discussion, bring children to be explicitly aware of the concepts.

• Discuss, model, and suggest effective problem-solving strategies such as figuring out exactly what the problem is, planning a solution, carrying out

the plan, checking the solution, and — always — monitoring progress.

• Have whole class discussions comparing the strategies of different groups along with the results of those strategies.

• Assist children, but only enough to get them going again. Use high-level (conscious, reflective) questioning and encourage high-level peer interaction.

• Help children to *make connections*: Demonstrate how problem-solving strategies and concepts developed on the computer can be used in other situations — in solving mathematical problems in and out of school.

• Maintain a balance between:

Teacher-directed activities and student-initiated projects.

Emphasis on product and process.

Accepting children's problem-solving strategies and guiding them to use more sophisticated processes.

• Allow children time to be engaged in and finish their projects.

• Encourage creativity and fantasy: Children might pretend the turtle is going on a trip; they might make up stories about their drawings, and so on.

• Help children become explicitly aware of their own reflective, mathematical thinking by asking them to explain, to you and to each other, what they are doing as well as how and why they are doing it.

Conclusion

We are learning how computers can be used to facilitate the development of mathematical thinking in young

children. Of course, there is still much to learn. We don't yet know how computers can *best* be used, which applications are best for which children, and what awaits us in the future.

We want to avoid unwise applications of computers, those that would replace (rather than complement) concrete experiences, *hurry* children, ignore their developmental level, or lead to verbalization without conceptual development.

To avoid these harmful applications and realize the potential of the promising ones, we need to establish principles and guidelines for using computers with the young child. The following are offered as a beginning:

• Recognize that there are situations in which computers SHOULD be used and there are situations in which computers SHOULD NOT be used (e.g., it is inappropriate to have young children do measurement activities on the computer; these should be concrete).

• Give priority to computer applications which place the children in the role of active learners with some control over their educational environment.

• Use child development as a guide (e.g., avoid programs that would require preschool children to keep multiple variables in mind all at once).

• Recognize that learning with computers should be a means to achieve educational goals, not an end.

• Choose computer applications that involve all facets of mathematics.

• Make mathematics meaningful — teach it as a system of concepts, relationships, and processes.

References

Clements, D. H. **Computers in Early and Primary Education**. Englewood Cliffs, NJ: Prentice-Hall, 1985.

Clements, D. H. "Research on Logo in Education: Is the Turtle Slow But Steady, or Not Even in the Race?," **Computers in the Schools**, 2, 55-71, 1985.

Kull, J. A. **Programming, Problem-solving, and Mathematical Learnings in Young Children Learning Logo: A Collaborative, Qualitative Study**. Paper presented at the annual meeting of the American Educational Research Association, April 1985.

Lawler, R. W. **Computer Experience and Cognitive Development: A Child's Learning in a Computer Culture**. New York: Halsted, Press, 1985.

Douglas H. Clements was an assistant professor in the early childhood department of Kent State University, teaching and conducting research in the area of computer applications in early childhood.

Photograph by Bonnie Neugebauer

Jackson Builds:
Making Mathematics Happen

based on an interview and observation with Martha Davis Perry and her son Jackson Perry by Dennie Palmer Wolf

Jackson is a builder: blocks, Legos, Construx — you name it, he does it for hours. One night, I realized I hadn't seen him in a long time, so I pushed open the door to his bedroom. There he was, sitting practically in the dark, in a forest of stars — small ones, medium ones, giant ones, all made from the pieces of his new construction set. When I looked closely, I saw that some of the largest stars had long single-piece arms and the arms in other ones were made of five or six short pieces. I thought, "That's interesting," but not much more.

Then several weeks later, he was sitting in the living room, trying to figure out how many hip-hip-hoorays we would say on our twins' second birthday — in our house, we say one hip-hip-hooray for every year. He kept going over it, "Hip-hip, hip-hip for Elizabeth, hip-hip, hip-hip for Tyler . . . hip-hip, hip-hip . . . hip-hip, hip-hip." But he couldn't figure out that it would be four all together. I listened and I remembered him building. He could figure out that two pieces would make a middle-sized arm, and that two middle-sized ones would make a long one, with no trial and error. But the counting or adding of two twos was very hard for him. It made me see how much math he's doing when he builds, at an age when he still finds numbers abstract and confusing.

That is Martha Davis Perry thinking out loud about her three year old son Jackson. Her story was intriguing and powerful, so we decided to watch Jackson building in order to track down just what kinds of early mathematical thinking are part and parcel of being a builder.

Sorting and Sets

Martha and Jackson sit side by side in the middle of the linoleum, literally surrounded by heaps of blocks. He says, "Put 'em all by the kinds, okay?"

Martha nods and helps by adding to the piles Jackson creates.

"Now by the colors — put the colored ones in this half here and the plain ones in the other half," he tells her.

Together, they divide their heaps into painted and plain wooden piles. Jackson waves a small red rectangle, "Only one red one, it's by itself."

Jackson works on until he finds a little doll and a marble, "Hey, Martha, this is silly."

"Yeah, this isn't a set of blocks, it's the set of everything that was ever on our living room floor!"

Jackson laughs and tosses the doll and the marble away from the blocks. "Get out of here, you guys."

Whether he knows it or not, Jackson is practicing two fundamental mathematical skills. First, he knows not to take things *just as they come*. He senses the importance of organizing his materials or information. As a builder, he decides that what matters most is shape. Here is where the second skill comes in — he carries out his organizing plan by sorting the blocks into rectangles, squares, and odd forms. Then he sorts those piles again by color.

His jokes about the lonely red rectangle and the doll and marble are sure signs that he is thinking carefully about *what belongs*. This is a skill that matters not just in sorting blocks. It is essential in counting, measuring, or estimating as well. If you are counting spoons, you have to stick to that set. It makes no sense to suddenly start including the forks and the glasses, too.

Measuring

Once the blocks are all laid out, Jackson sits back.

"What are you going to build?"

"Don't know."

"Maybe a cherry picker, you've built some good cherry pickers before."

"Yeah . . . but I need wheels and there aren't any ones here."

"I bet you could find some. Have a look."

Jackson rakes through the piles and pulls out a wooden barrel shape. He continues searching, pausing over a slender column, but then puts it back. At last he holds up a much thicker column, "Okay, now, there's two wheels."

He puts the barrel and the column on their sides and lays a flat board across them. "See, they both work."

He rummages in the blocks looking for more wheels, but has no luck. "This won't work, there aren't enough wheels . . . see no wheels for here and here." Jackson points to where the back pair of wheels would have gone. "So, no cherry picker, I don't think."

Here Jackson is working on the notion of finding a match or an equivalent. He is deciding — in his mind — that the first column is too small to match the barrel. Although he is doing it in terms of physical size, he may be building an important foundation for an understanding of the concept of equals, as in 1 + 3 = 4 or 1 yard = 3 feet.

He is also doing a different sort of measuring. When he decides he hasn't enough wheels to complete his cherry picker, he's exercising the ability to measure his current efforts against an outcome he had in mind. This is a capacity that's vital to judging where you are, whether you are *on track*, if you have enough information or materials to complete a job. He also measures the various ramps against his idea for *just the right ramp* in the next few moments:

Jackson lays down two squares, tops them with a rectangle, and adds an arch-shaped block on top. Interestingly, the blocks are all the same length. "A bridge . . . the cargo could go through the hole, but then it needs to get down." Jackson searches for blocks that will make a ramp from the arch opening down to the floor. He skips over ones that are clearly too long or short and collects several possible blocks in a small pile. One after another, he tries them. All of them work as ramps, but some make a steep ramp, while others create a gentler incline. "Too steep . . . still too steep . . . this one is okay."

Operations and Rules

At this point, Jackson builds a large, spidery-looking spaceship from his Construx (a snap-together building set).

"How about a garage for that spaceship?" asks Martha.

"No spaceships don't have garages . . . just cars."

"Right, not garages, they call them silos. But something to keep it from getting rusty. See, we could make a floor like this." She lays down four flat planks.

Jackson inspects her work. "No, not so good. It has this little bump." He points to a gap between the floor and the edge of the plank. "The spaceship will push it when it tries to roll in."

"Well, you could be the crane to lift it in — or you could use the Construx to build a crane."

Satisfied he can settle the problem *down the road*, Jackson begins to put up walls. He works in a pattern: one block on the left side, the back, the right side. He continues until he has a building that is four blocks tall on three sides. "No more, it might crash."

He lifts the ship into the building, lowering it very gently into position. "Fits — just — no a little bit too long."

He carefully adds another plank to the floor, sliding it under the wheels of the ship. "NOW! NOW! Martha, look."

"You did it. Think it needs a roof? You know, like our garage has a roof to keep the car dry?"

"No, I told you, spaceships don't have garages. And see the spaceship already has one roof, it doesn't need two. Besides, look . . . ." (He suspends one of the longest blocks over the building, showing her that it will not span the distance.)

"How about a smokestack?" Martha stacks five small square blocks up the outside of the building.

"It's not big enough. Needs to be bigger."

"Bigger?"

"Yeah, it's for a big spaceship." Jackson begins building a second stack out of rectangular blocks. "If I use bigger blocks, it will be quicker."

"What? How come?"

"They go up faster." He stacks three long rectangles, end on end. The result is a stack that towers over the first one. "Oops, too tall." Jackson subtracts one rectangle, but that leaves the second stack shorter than the first. "I can't."

"You've done it before — find some blocks to make it work."

Jackson stares down at his piles of squares and shorter rectangles. His hand darts down and picks up a square. He sets it atop the stack of two rectangles and laughs as he sees that it just matches the first stack.

In addition to organizing and measuring, Jackson is working with the block builder's equivalent of mathematical operations like adding and subtracting. For example, he adds one level to his silo by placing one more block to each side and the back. He also experiments with a transformation which is very much like subtraction, taking away a block when he sees that the smokestack is too high. The varied block sizes prompt him to work on the problem of adding and subtracting different units (e.g., a square or a longer rectangle) — just as, when working with numerals, he might have to anticipate the very different effects of adding 2 or 5 to 10.

When Jackson announces that using bigger blocks makes the stack build up *quicker*, he is doing some very sophisticated thinking aloud about the ways in which quantities can be transformed. Rather than thinking just about the particular squares and rectangles at hand, he is thinking about the general case. In essence, he is noticing a general pattern: *It takes a lot of little ones to do what a few big ones do.* That kind of broad thinking is what underlies understanding and formulating mathematical principles or rules.

Comparisons, Dimensions, and Relationships

Jackson picks up a ball and begins to move it through the scene he's created. "See, this can go up here . . . uh uh uh (sound effects of pushing a ball up the ramp with lots of effort) . . . through the cargo hole, then down the other side . . . wheeeeeee!!!" (sound effects of a ball rolling effortlessly down the ramp).

He guides the ball onto the back of the spaceship. "Now it can start up." He touches the three smokestacks. "This makes more smoke than cars. That's why it needs these three big ones."

"More smoke than cars? Why?"

"Cause it flies and cars don't."

"Yeah?"

"When you fly, you have to go up more."

"Hmmmm."

"The man inside needs a chair so he can get out of the spaceship and look to see if it's windy." (Jackson builds one inside the building.)

"Why does he want to look?"

"Cause the wind makes it hard to fly."

He places a stack of blocks on the opposite wall and then adds a control panel from his Construx set. "Now the radio is up more."

"How come it has to be up?"

"It's better that way — cause then . . . cause then the man's voice doesn't have to go so far to get to the spaceship when it's flying."

"Can't he just make it go louder?"

"Yeah, they can make their voices go louder so it can go up and reach where the spaceship is, even if it's raining."

He holds the ship aloft above the building. "See, now the spaceship can hear him, even if he's talking soft, cause it's not raining. Cause it's not raining, they don't need so much loudness."

Even the sound effects Jackson makes suggest he understands another basic mathematical concept: the idea of a dimension, or a gradient, along with items or events can be compared. Earlier in his block play, he explored making steeper and not-so-steep ramps. In this segment, Jackson comes back to thinking about these kinds of comparisons and relationships. With his voice he compares a steep ascent and a rolling descent: going up is hard; sliding down is easy.

But Jackson goes beyond such simple comparisons when he begins to think aloud about the whys behind such relationships. He explains that cars make a little and spaceships make a lot of smoke because the ships have to work harder. He continues to reason that more smoke demands more stacks. At that moment he is exploring the relationships across the dimensions of little-to-much work, little-to-lots of smoke, and numbers of stacks. He pursues this line of thinking when he thinks about how the distance from ship to ground, the presence or absence of rain, and the loudness or softness of the operator's voice might all interact.

Photograph by Bonnie Neugebauer

While Jackson is not yet writing equations or drawing graphs, he is laying the foundation for some fundamental mathematical understandings about the connections between quantities. (Such understandings underlie much of natural science and statistics: As the number of trees declines in an urban area, what happens to wildlife? As the cost of providing child care increases, and the size of federal support declines, what happens to enrollment?)

Joking Around

Jackson slides the spaceship back into its building. "I want to make a crane to lift it in and out of the building." He works on building an arm with a hook, but runs out of steam before he completes any kind of body for the arm. "I will just use it this way." He lowers the hook to the ship, attaches it, and lifts it all slowly skywards. "I am the crane lifting a crane," he jokes.

"Maybe there needs to be a crane to lift me, too. A crane to lift a crane to lift a crane."

Jackson and Martha aren't involved in a mathematics tutoring session; there is no set of facts or concepts they must move through in their half hour together. Instead, they more or less invent interesting mathematical problems as they go, such as their effort to build three equal stacks out of different sized blocks. There is also the freedom to fool around — remember their joke about the doll discovered among the blocks.

Far from being *just silly*, these kinds of jokes often clinch an idea that Jackson and Martha have been exploring. The joke marks the arrival of understanding — an idea is so firmly in mind, it can be played with. In the example just above, the joke about a crane lifting a crane lifting a crane may be an early exploration of the idea that things might go on forever — the concept of infinity.

Errors and Differences

"I think I'm through with the station, I want to build more on the spaceship." With that, Jackson dismantles his original ship and builds a larger, spidery-shaped one with long-jointed legs and wheels. After he snaps the last wheel into place, he flips the ship upright. "A new spaceship!" But then he notices that the ship wobbles. He checks each leg, making sure it has the same number of pieces and that the wheels are all the same size.

"Hmm, why is this thing tippy? I can't see." He lies down flat on his stomach and looks at the ship from the underside. "Maybe . . . maybe it's this propeller . . . it's heavy. Maybe it hangs down and makes it wobble. You think so?" he asks looking over.

"I don't know. You could take it off and see if it works."

"No, it needs its propeller." Jackson is through — for the moment — with rigorous testing; he is more interested in getting on with things. He rolls the ship across the floor, untroubled by the fact that one leg lifts slightly off the ground. He parks in the garage and looks around.

Martha notices the pause. "Maybe that ship could move these blocks — like cargo."

"No, you need a grabber."

"Like we saw the construction workers using?"

"Yeah, but grabbers can't move square things, just like pipes."

"Oh, I think they can adjust their pincers and pick up square things."

"No, too heavy."

"They're strong pieces of machinery, I bet they could do it."

"I think they might break and then there'd be no one to lift the pipes."

"Maybe. We should look when we go by there again."

As Jackson builds, not everything goes as planned. Construction (like mathematics later) involves backtracking, checking, and reflecting. *Did I really put three short pieces on all the legs?* But at three, Jackson has only some interest in testing out his theories. Martha respects this — she doesn't tell him that his theory about the propeller is wrong or that he must track down what's wrong with the ship.

Moreover, building (like much serious problem solving) involves areas of opinion and places for discussion. It

isn't all known procedures and right answers. Jackson and Martha don't agree about what a grabber can do, and they have frank differences of opinion about just how strong it is. As Jackson talks through his point of view, he comes closer and closer to being able to say just what he thinks the grabber can and can't do. In a way, his differences with Martha may help him to explore and crystallize his thoughts.

Good Partnerships and Raw Materials

Jackson is not just building cargo ramps and spaceships, he is building an understanding of some basic mathematical concepts like *equals*, *more*, and *less*. He is also literally constructing an understanding of mathematical processes by adding to, taking away, matching, comparing, and measuring his structures.

But Jackson isn't working in a vacuum. He has a colleague in Martha: someone who offers (but doesn't insist on) ideas, asks him to explain what's on his mind, puts in her *two cents* (but lets him draw his own conclusions).

In his blocks and Construx pieces, he has some of the best raw materials for early mathematical learning. They provide him with concrete examples of the ways that sets, units, relationships, and transformations look, feel, and work. Between his interested partner and such good raw materials, Jackson has what might be thought of as a grade-A laboratory for early mathematical thinking.

Martha Davis Perry was a researcher working at the Harvard Graduate School of Education. Her children — Jackson, Elizabeth, and Tyler — made mathematics happen all the time: with blocks, Legos, peas, you name it.

Idea Sparkers: Small But Powerful Ways to Teach Mathematical Thinking

by Virginia Haugen and Bonnie Neugebauer

Building a math-rich environment for young children is up to you. And it can be great fun. We've put our heads together — *two* heads are better than *one*! — and come up with all sorts of sparks, seeds, germs of ideas for enriching the environment you create.

Our purpose is not to give directions, rather to spur your own creativity. And always it is our intent that the enrichment be there for the child to discover, rather than the teacher to teach. Let's get on with it — through the day with numbers:

Arrivals — Taking Off

Coat Match. Before hats and coats are put away, have children find someone who matches them — color of jacket, type of boots or lunch box, or shape of hat. Then off they go together to put things away. (This is also a good way to get socializing off to a good start in the morning.)

Arrival Plane. Create an arrival train with numbered cars — or better yet the inside of an airplane with numbered seats. Each car/seat is a pocket which holds a child's photograph and name (laminated or covered in clear contact paper). As children come in, they collect their own photos from the storage pocket and place them in order in the seats. It's easy for both children and

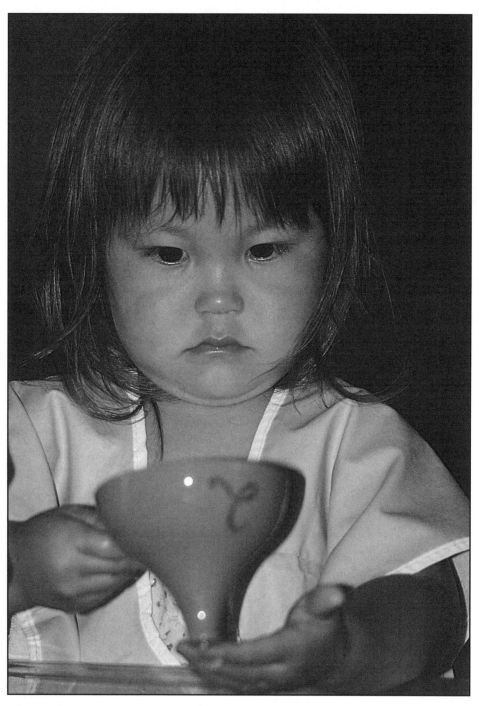

Photograph by Bonnie Neugebauer

Clothing Graph. Have children graph outdoor clothing as they arrive. They place their pictures in columns which correspond to what they're wearing — coats with zippers, coats with buttons (or numbers of buttons), colors of hats, mittens or no mittens.

Number Words. Use number vocabulary during arrival times — *You're the first one here! Mary was here before you, so you're second.*

Activity Timeline. Create a clothesline timeline (child eye level) of the daily routine with separate cards symbolizing or picturing (photos are even better) each activity. As the activity ends, children turn the cards around to the blank side and pin them back up. This timeline provides a visual sense of the progress of the day. It can also be a way of recording group choices.

Calendar. Curtain hooks centered on a poster board provide an easy-to-make calendar. Dates (written on formica chips) hang in a pile until they are individually added to the calendar. Patterns can be added by planning alternating colors of formica chips or by adding symbols next to the date.

Flip Calendar. A flip chart calendar using block outline numbers can be done in two ways (at least) to highlight the particular day. As a planning device, it is done the last day of the preceding month with children decorating the numbers as they wish (birthday children get their own day). One child's artwork is spotlighted each day of the coming month; anticipation mounts.

As a diary of classroom happenings, the individually numbered pages are decorated throughout the day as children think of events they want to record or highlight. As the month ends, this flip chart becomes a journal of what happened in the lives of this

adults to see how many children are still on their way and how many are out for the day. (The train/airplane can be used as a helper device throughout the day — *Will the child in seat #5 please find the crayons?*)

Photo Reductions. Throughout we will suggest using photos of the children. It's a great way to use those small school photographs; otherwise, you can take a set yourself (Baratta-Lorton). Photocopy and reduce them to assorted sizes (certain photocopy machines can do such things), laminate and use them in all sorts of wonderful ways such as:

Sorting Children

My daughter's terrific third grade teacher had a poster up in her room — 101 Ways to Line Up (other than by sex). Here it is adapted as ways to sort young children.

By Clothing:

kind of shirts
colors of socks
jeans or non-jeans
shoe styles or colors
belted and unbelted
collars and collarless
stripes and no stripes
short sleeves or long sleeves

By Identifying:

right and left
before and after
animal and insect sounds
pennies, nickels, dimes, quarters
shapes
other children by name

Numerically by:

initial letter in name
syllables in name
number of buttons/pockets
multiples of 2, 3, 5, 10
digits of phone number
number of brothers and sisters
birthday month

Alphabetically by:

Z to A
last name
first name
father's name
mother's name

By Favorite:

sport • hero/heroine • movie
sandwich • flower • book
season • song • animal
game • vegetable • color
ice cream • sound

particular group of children. And as the volumes accumulate, a real feeling of the passage of time, of accomplishment, can develop.

Circle Time — Numbers in the Square

Talking Math. Does it add new interest to the routine if circle time becomes square time or triangle time or zigzag time? Number discussions become uncorrected responses to such inquiries as: *What's the highest number you can think of? How do you learn numbers? How do you think numbers started? What is a number?* (Chenfeld)

Surveys. This is an excellent opportunity for surveys — *How many things do you see that come in pairs? Let's sort our shoes* (one comes off, one stays on) *into rows of shoes with laces, shoes with velcro, shoes for pulling on.*

Guess Again. Each child has a pile of five fish crackers (raisins). Everyone covers eyes except one child who hides some of the fish crackers in his hand. The others, now looking, guess how many crackers are hidden in his hand (remainder are in full view).

Fill-Me Bags. Lunch bags, marked *Fill Me with 2 Things* (or more) are sent home. Each child shares the contents of his bag, then records the contents by drawing pictures on the bag. Sort the collections by various characteristics. Create patterns with the collections, predicting what comes next. *What two things take up the smallest space? the largest?* When collections are back in the bags, children try to remember the contents.

Just Right Chart. Design a chart with columns marked *too many, too few, just right.* Children bring in collections of things, then a die is rolled to determine the *just right* number of items for that day. As each child shows his collection, the items are counted, and the child's picture is entered in the appropriate column.

Questions Game. Children guess contents of another child's bag, allowing only five (or whatever) guesses. Tally guesses.

Snacktime — Edible Numbers

Peanut Hunt. Everyone covers eyes and holds out the other hand to receive a *special* number of peanuts. Children count their peanuts. Open peanuts to find one with just one nut inside. Then two. Any with three? (If you don't want the children to eat peanuts, try it with raisins.) (Chenfeld) *How will you eat them? One at a* *time? Two at a time? Three? Can you find the little man inside the peanut? Does every peanut have one?*

Fishy Story. Each child takes four fish crackers. *A big, hungry whale is coming! He eats two of your little fish! Oh, there are only three left!* (Sometimes teachers can *make mistakes.* Children love to be the authority.)

Snack Graph. Children can easily indicate their choice for snack (Ritz crackers or Wheat Thins) by placing their picture inside the shape which corresponds to their favorite cracker.

Carrot Puzzles. Children (or teachers) cut a carrot into three (or more) pieces, scramble them, and try to fit the carrot back together. (Brown)

How many ways can you cut a banana/apple to get different shapes? Can you predict what you will see? How many segments will an orange have? Do oranges always have the same number of segments?

Going Outdoors — Natural Numbers

Inventory. Make an inventory of what you will need — a pair of mittens for a pair of hands, one coat for one body, one hat for one head. . . .

Groups. Children can form groups or lines according to their outer wear — coats with zippers, coats with buttons, numbers of buttons, hats and no hats. Which group is largest?

Pocket Fillers. What amount or number of something will fill your pocket? (Provide an assortment of nuts ranging in size from acorn to coconut, or balls of different sizes.)

Classroom Model. How many different ways are there to walk from the classroom to the playground? A card-

board model of the classroom can be great for *working out* many things. Here children can map out their paths with fingers and then try to walk the same path through the classroom. (Forman and Hill)

How many giant steps do we take to cross the playground? What does our path look like?

Natural World. Find things that have two parts, three parts. Make collections of rocks, leaves, litter.

Naptimes — Alternatives to Counting Sheep

Choose two small things (one round thing, three square things) to take to your mat.

Can you lay your mats out in the shape of a square? A circle? Can you lay your mats in groups of two? How about three? Can you put your mat near (beside, on, between, next to) _____?

How many parts of your body are touching the mat? When you are comfortable, what shape does your body make? Is there another comfortable shape for your body?

Let's count the shoes we've lined up in pairs. When I point to the first shoe, let's cover our mouths so that no one can hear us. When I point to the second shoe, whisper the number. (Alternations continue.)

Backrubs can be varied in shape and direction — *Today I'm giving circle rubs* (wiggly line rubs, up and down rubs, long and short rubs).

Cleanup — A Clean Sweep

Wouldn't it be great to have a real time clock for children to use to punch in and out throughout the day

as they start and finish activities? As computers replace other office/factory equipment, many of these wonderful machines have to be landing in the dump.

Let's all put away five things, all the round things, everything that isn't round (pretty tricky).

Let's work in s-l-o-w — m-o-t-i-o-n. Whoops, I feel myself speeding up. . . .

Making hourglasses of different sizes with the children can provide a great activity as well as a visual device for helping children develop understandings of the passage of time. (All you need are pairs of discarded glass/plastic containers, sand/beans/popcorn, and epoxy.) If you create a variety of these hourglasses, children can choose the one they feel is more appropriate for timing a specific activity and try to *beat the clock.*

Transitions — Waiting Games

Shape Up. Use number vocabulary to challenge children to do various tricks with their bodies: *Put your toes higher than your head. Hold up a few fingers.* (Chenfeld)

Keeping in Touch. In partners, children take turns touching each others' backs and guessing. *Is the touch with few fingers or many fingers? Long or short? High or low?*

Top Ten. Sing a song selected from the class created list of *Top Ten Favorites.* (Chenfeld)

Magic Finger Tricks. *All fingers disappear. How many shall we make appear? Can our fingers make a circle? a square? something tiny? something big?* (Chenfeld)

Clap, Clap, Pop. On the *pop*, everyone holds up one to five fingers.

Counting and grouping or just excitement can follow.

Lucky Guesses. *Can you guess how many things are in my pocket? That's too many or that's too few* (until children guess correct number).

Celebrations —
The Joy of Numbers

Lucky Number Day. Everyone selects a lucky number. *Draw a picture showing your lucky number in as many ways as you can. Shall we guess what lucky number is "hidden" in this picture? Collect pieces from the scrap box or wood box to equal your lucky number — make a collage or construction with them. Create a pattern using colored squares with your lucky number. Can you repeat the pattern?* (Chenfeld)

Number 4 Day. Make a shape holding hands in groups of four children. Hop across the room in your shape. Can you keep the shape without holding hands as you come back? (Gilbert) Talk about four, write it, count it. Draw pictures of four things on paper and cut into the shape of the number 4. Make up a song about four, a puppet show, a mobile. Dance in groups of four, repeating each step four times. Paint with four colors. Draw pictures with four trees, four circles, four people. Make a picture with four selections from the scrounge box.

Birthdays. Write a recipe for the birthday child: *To make an Angela, you need one happy face, two legs, 85 giggles, one body, a million running steps. . . . Matthew is five today. What gifts can we give him in fives? — five smiles, five hugs, five ear wiggles, five claps. . . .* (Chenfeld)

Giant Day. Large paper tubes stacked from floor to ceiling create the giant's legs. With the addition of box shoes, his presence is evident. *How*

long would the giant's shoelaces have to be? What would things look like from way up there? Oversizing everything throughout the day can be a source of wonder and excitement, as well as a learning activity. Oversized cracker or muffin for snack. Juice from a bucket. Let your imagination run wild!

Doll's Tea Party. Here's an opportunity to marvel at tiny things, as miniatures are served for snack in the tea party set and children construct tiny things for their dolls (or teddies).

And what about days in which everything is doubled or tripled or divided into halves, thirds, or quarters?

Other Terrific Ideas:
We Couldn't Stop Ourselves

Create an obstacle course either numbering the stations or using shapes to climb over, around, and through. Use spatial relations words as you cheer children on. Children can use their bodies to create the obstacles as well as to surmount them.

Put and Take. Make a cube with the letter *P* marked on three sides and the letter *T* on the other three. Each child has a pile of three (or more) fish crackers; there's a larger pile of crackers in the middle. If the child rolls a *P* with the cube, she *puts* a cracker into the center. If she rolls a *T*, she *takes* one from the center.

Making Books with Children. Telephone or address book (use the photocopied pictures for identification), recipe book for classroom cooking project, "I Know These Numbers," "Things That Come in Pairs," "My Lucky Number Book," "The Most," "The Tiniest."

Imaginary Recipes. These can either be real-life inventories or fantasies (which give children an opportunity to use large numbers). Let's write a

recipe for a steamroller (a day, a person). (Chenfeld)

Field Trips can be rich in math potential. For millions of ideas — **Yellow Pages of Learning Resources**, Richard Saul Wurman (ed.), The MIT Press, Cambridge, MA 02142.

References

Baratta-Lorton, Mary. **Mathematics Their Way.** Menlo Park, CA: Addison-Wesley Publishing Company, 1976.

Brown, Sam Ed. **One, Two, Buckle My Shoe** (illustrated by Jula Libonn). Beltsville, MD: Gryphon House, 1982.

Chenfeld, Mimi Brodsky. **Creative Activities for Young Children.** San Diego, CA: Harcourt Brace Jovanovich, 1983.

Forman, George E., and Fleet Hill. **Constructive Play.** Menlo Park, CA: Addison-Wesley Publishing Company, 1984.

Gilbert, Anne Green. **Teaching the Three Rs Through Movement Experiences.** Burgess Publishing Company, 7108 Ohms Lane, Minneapolis, MN 55435, 1977.

Virginia Haugen, Tacoma, Washington, has sparked countless ideas and learning experiences in her work as art, elementary, and Montessori teacher; preschool teacher/director; and mother and grandmother.

Bonnie Neugebauer is the editor of **Child Care Information Exchange***.*

Numbers, Numbers Everywhere: Make Your Child Aware

A Hand-Out for Parents

As parents, we have so many opportunities to create in our children an awareness of numbers as part of everyday life — an exciting part as well as necessary!

Make your conversations rich with math vocabulary — wonderings. *(I wonder if there's a box this present can fit into. I wonder how many pairs of socks are in the wash . . . who had the most pairs. I wonder if you weigh more in your pajamas or in your snowsuit.)*

Rather than correct your child's number attempts, **ask questions to encourage further exploration** or self correction. *(Count again and see if you get the same number.)*

Inventories or hunts can be fun. *How many pairs of brown shoes are in our house? How many windows do we have? . . . doors? What couldn't fit in our door?* Show your child the tally method for keeping count (HHH 11). *How many light switches? — single, double, triple? What things in our house have numbers on them? Why are these numbers on them?*

Encourage your child to make collections of rocks, stamps, button, lids, keys. Compare and sort them by color. *Can you think of another way to sort (shape, size)?* Estimate how many or how much of something will fit. *Was your estimate too few/ too many/just right?* Create designs and patterns with the collections.

Play commercial as well as homemade games. Help your child create her own board game using a spinner or dice for moves and drawing with permanent markers on a piece of shower curtain to make the gameboard.

Feel free to let your young child create his own rules. **Allow negotiation** between children when there are disagreements about rules, letting them solve the problem if possible. This promotes thinking skills as they reason out their own positions.

Make a cardboard dollhouse of your own with your child. This helps your child understand spacial relationships.

Develop a chart of *Things Happening Today.* Talk about what you'll do first, last, etc. It might be fun to do this with photographs or to let your child draw the pictures.

Including children in household chores makes them feel important and needed, and it provides opportunities for number activities.

• Setting the table: Inexpensive plastic placemats with silver, glasses, plates, and napkins outlined with black permanent marker insures success on the job.

Use Math Words

large	infinity	light
small	more	heavy
full	less	up
empty	a lot	down
first	little	out
second	big	forward
third	same	backward
fourth	different	sideways
last	equal	short
under	single	bottom
over	double	tall
around	triple	next
through	high	many
beside	low	few
behind	whole	narrow
above	half	some
between	all	circle
below	none	square
front	wide	rectangle
middle	nothing	in
back	everything	

1 2 3 4 5 6

• Laundry: Sorting by color (light/dark), size, family member; matching by pairs; measuring soap.

• Grocery shopping: Helping make the list, identifying, matching with coupons, counting the number of items.

• Picking up: Pick up round things, five little things, don't pick up blue things.

• Cooking: Measuring, counting, estimating, shape making, and tasting, too.

Let your imagination wander!

Mollie, Barney, Stuart, and I: The Social and Emotional Side of Numbers

an interview with Vivian Gussin Paley by Dennie Palmer Wolf

For a teacher, the task of figuring out what three year olds know and don't know about such concepts as number and space is like putting together a puzzle in which the shapes keep changing. Or maybe it is like playing a game in which the rules keep shifting.

The tendency of threes, and even fours, to repeat little pieces of memorized data may fool adults into premature expectations and cause even the most experienced teacher to be unsure of her role. "Is this a teaching moment?" she wonders, "Or shall the child be in charge of this event?"

When It's Pretend, You Don't Need to Teach

Mollie, age three, calls off numbers in fast succession, as if really counting. She tells me the number of brushes, 1 to 15, while I line them up in paint jars. In her rapid calculations, she misses a few brushes at the start and adds a few at the end. But I don't attempt to make her count correctly. Her job is to see that all the jars have brushes. There is no practical reason to count brushes; and she is, in effect, pretending to count. As her teacher, I listen carefully so that I may learn something new about Mollie.

The games we play at the play dough table involve similar kinds of pretend mathematics. The rules are Mollie's.

"Make me a bird's nest," is the way she begins one of her games.

"How many eggs does a mother bird lay?" I must then ask.

"Six, only six," she says.

"Here they are," I say, dropping the eggs into place. "How many eggs are there, Mollie?"

"One, two, three," she counts, holding her fingers over two eggs at a time. I have already learned that if I correct her and ask her to count again I am spoiling the game. It is her game and she wants to be in control. For the remainder of today's game she counts to five, no matter how many eggs are in the nest.

"I understand your game, Mollie," I say. "You are calling all the egg piles a five, right?"

She nods happily, unaware that she is being *taught* a lesson in logical analysis.

There is no necessary connection in Mollie's game between her eggs and the words called numbers. But I notice that she assembles her four snack crackers daily without error. Snack time is, in fact, a good time for real counting. When Barney takes three crackers, I ask him if he is not hungry, since he has taken one less than he is allowed. We all count Barney's crackers and decide he must take another. Those who take more than four are quickly censured by the others. Again, we must count. It is a social issue.

Another time, we are preparing for a visit to an ice cream parlor; and we must order in advance the correct number of vanilla, chocolate, and strawberry scoops. Since each serving will cost 40 cents ("Is that a lot much?" asks Mollie), we cannot make a mistake. We count raised hands once, and then a second time. It is an economic issue.

The question the teacher must ask then is: Are we dealing with a real problem in which numerical accuracy is important or can the child's game be the governing standard?

Here are Mollie and Margaret in the doll corner playing hospital.

"That one is the sick baby. Give her six, four, one blue vitamins."

"One, two, six, four. . . . There, all better."

"No, my baby is too sick because she eated too much candy. Give her fourteen, twenty-two."

I would no more correct Mollie's counting here than drill her on saying *ate* rather than *eated*.

Social Mathematics: When to Let Children Teach Counting

Later, in the block area, the girls are in real need of numerical assistance.

"Teacher, Mollie is taking my blocks!" Margaret complains.

But Mollie is adamant. "She has too much than I have," Mollie pouts, examining her large collection which is at least twice the size of Margaret's.

"Not more," Margaret argues, "only four more."

Neither girl can judge the relative size of her structures.

Photograph by Judy Burr

Photograph by Judy Burr

three, four," she counts out the blocks and places them on Mollie's structure.

Mollie brightens. Four blocks from an older child are easily worth 17 from any other source.

"Margaret, want to be my baby bunny?" Mollie asks, "and live in my house?" It is easier to share blocks when you share a fantasy.

Social Geometry Between Children

Meanwhile, two feet away, another controversy explodes, and once again it has as much to do with physical perception as social readiness.

"He's making his blocks go on my ship!" Barney screams. "I keep telling him not to."

"I'm making a ship, too," Stuart says.

"Why not connect your ships?" I ask.

"I don't want to," Barney says.

"Well, then, could you build your ship in that other direction, Stuart?" I suggest.

Stuart nods, then places two more blocks against Barney's ship.

"See, he's doing it again!" Barney cries.

"See if you can help him, Barney. He is having trouble doing it."

Barney starts to rearrange the blocks, only to find himself retracing Stuart's error. The two boys can no more change the direction of the existing structure than control the lines they draw on a piece of paper. Once again, it is time to call in an older child. Maybe one of them can teach Stuart something about the kind of geometry you need to work together.

"But Mollie," I say, "you already have more than Margaret."

"No, I don't." Mollie's eyes fill at my suggestion that she is wrong. "Margaret has to give me nine blocks."

Mollie remembers an unused rule created by the older children. It states: "If you are using all the blocks and others want to build, give them nine." What she cannot see is that her friend has fewer than nine blocks for her entire building. If she cannot see it, it is useless for me to point it out.

"Tell you what," I say, "why don't you each decide how many more blocks you need, and we'll ask Libby if you can borrow some." Part of my teaching job is to know when it is other children, not me, or another adult, who can provide this assistance. Libby, a five year old, has the sense of what nine blocks look like, but she doesn't overwhelm fantasy with fact, as I might.

"I need 17," Mollie says.

"I'll give you four," Libby tells her. "Seventeen is too much. One, two,

I could alter the ship's direction myself far more efficiently; but the four and five year old helpers, being only one or two steps up the developmental ladder, will be far better teachers and may even help extend the plot. I notice that when I step in to bring quick order to the mathematical complexity of the block area, my extra measure of neatness often puts a damper on the fantasy play that is going on.

"Erik, can you help Stuart turn his ship around so it won't bump into Barney's?" I ask a nearby four year old.

"Just make it go up, up, up, Stuart." Erik decides quickly. "It's a rocket, right? Put that block here to make it pointy. I'm the driver, okay? Call me Luke."

One Teacher's Social Geometry

Stuart envisions the transformation easily; but before Erik can climb aboard, Christopher comes tunneling through both space ships as if they were not there. He is the one three year old boy who has good control over lines and shapes, block building, and counting.

But social boundaries and other kinds of design must require entirely different kinds of perception, and Christopher has not yet learned to stop before entering someone else's territory. He happens to be an expert counter and block builder, yet he does not know how to say, "Can I play?" Just as it is easier to share blocks when you share a fantasy game, boundary lines are more visible if you have a role to play inside the spaceship.

Finding a role in the ship for someone who has just knocked down one of its walls is beyond any child's skills. It requires a teacher's best efforts.

"If Christopher builds a nice straight wall, could he be the second navigator?" I ask. "You know he's a good builder. I'll help you, Christopher, if it's too hard."

"It's not too hard," he replies. As second navigator he has a good reason to maintain straight walls.

But what does all this socialization have to do with teaching math concepts? A great deal, for the consistent message in early childhood education must be that the world is a well-ordered place in which logical behavior is the goal wherever possible.

When Teaching Numbers Isn't Really the Point

If numbers and shapes are part of the social order, so, too, can they enter into the language of feelings, such as those about growing bigger.

"I'm tall, Maria. Look how tall I am. I'm getting taller. We're the same tall."

"Uh-uh, Mollie, I am five and you are only three."

"I"m taller, Maria. Every day I eat."

"But I'm this tall, Mollie, and you're not."

"I'm this tall, too. I'm five inches," Mollie says.

"No, you're not."

Mollie is crying. "I'm already four inches bigger. Teacher," Maria says, "I'm not too tall."

"You're a tall three year old," I say.

"I'm a five-incher," she sobs.

"You were a five-incher, I bet, when you were Fire Star in the blocks."

Mollie smiles. "Fire Star really is a five-incher," she announces.

Teachers cannot legislate the separation of fantasy from fact in early childhood, nor should they wish to. A *five-incher Fire Star* is more real to Mollie than the five inch mark on the ruler. And *fourteen, twenty-two* has the proper sound of bigness needed for the doll corner and the blocks. Any one number alone doesn't seem quite big enough.

A year later, when Mollie is four, I still cannot teach her facts which she does not already know. She is now a good counter up to ten and can call off Rainbow Brite's horses in accurate formation: "First Starlite, second Starlite, third Starlite, fourth, and five-eth." However, her ordinal concepts are notably idiosyncratic.

Teaching Is Listening

When Mollie tells me she lives on the first floor, I am confused, since I have visited her in a third floor apartment. Perhaps she has moved. "Don't you still live at the top of all the stairs, Mollie, near the roof?" "Yes, it is called the first floor," she says.

"Then what is the bottom floor called?" I ask. "Where the mail boxes are."

"That's . . . that's . . . that's . . . We call that the fourth floor," she replies.

"Here, Mollie, let me draw you a picture of your building." I get out the crayons and make a sketch. "Now point to your windows."

She puts her finger on the top row of windows. "Here is my window where I sleep."

"We call that the third floor, Mollie."

"No, because don't you know, my house

only has one floor in it? It's already on the first floor. And the other floors they call it other people's houses."

"Ahh . . . I see, because your house is all on one floor, you call that the first floor. Your apartment doesn't have a second or a third floor in it."

"Right," Mollie says, pleased that I understand.

Her error surprises me. She counts out Rainbow Brite's horses so easily now, I expect her to understand that her third floor is the same third that she uses to count horses. But, clearly, counting horses and naming floors do not necessarily go by the same rules. One day, of course, she will wake up knowing the rules are the same, and it is not necessary or useful to drill her on it now.

Why not insist that Mollie call it the third floor? She is an agreeable child who will surely say "third" if it pleases the teacher. She will say it and not believe it, or she will think it does not matter whether or not she understands and lose faith in her own judgments.

A Few Words About Teaching

As Mollie's teacher, I do not want her to think she must always take my view of what is true, that knowledge is something coming from me alone. Rote memorization is not to become Mollie's definition of learning — nor mine. I must have enough faith in the learning process to be patient, to wait for her to reach the next level in her own time.

We teachers are not here to model answers; one cannot, in fact, model an answer. We can, however, model a process of logical thinking and a strong curiosity about how others arrive at their own thoughts.

Idea: Supportive Environment

Jan Bandich, Head Start, **Riverside County Superintendent of Schools**, Riverside, California:

A supportive environment in which a child can have time to freely explore and experiment with different solutions is as important for children as is the access to a variety of materials and activities. An atmosphere that supports each child's individual accomplishment fosters learning through discovery.

An attitude of "How many ways can you think of to show 5?" or "Let's see how many ways we can think of to move our bodies in a circle" provides a more open-ended, divergent mode of thinking for a child than "Everyone circle all the sets of three with a red crayon" or "This is how to make a 4."

Facilitators need to be sensitive to what children are thinking and experiencing to be able to ascertain what the child's understandings are in order to help extend and expand their concepts.

"Do you have more big shells or more small shells?"

"What could you do so that there would be more red blocks than blue ones?"

"How could you make the mercury on the thermometer go up? Go down? Why?"

"Tell me about your set of shells. Why did you put these here and those there?"

"Which do you think is longer? How could you find out?"

Opportunities to verbalize their observations help children think through and extend what they are experiencing.

There are math concepts all around children every day; facilitators need to expand their own thinking to include all types of mathematical thinking — temporal, spatial, measurement, classification, as well as those of quantity and counting.

Children need a multitude of hands-on experiences to build math frameworks before they are developmentally ready for the more symbolic reading and writing of numerals and computations.

Books by Vivian Gussin Paley

White Teacher (Harvard University Press, 1979).

Wally's Stories (Harvard University Press, 1981).

Boys and Girls: Superheroes in the Doll Corner (University of Chicago Press, 1984).

Mollie is Three: Growing Up in School (University of Chicago Press, Spring 1986) — on which her interview is based.

Vivian Gussin Paley is retired from the preschool of the University of Chicago Laboratory School. She is the author of several books about teaching and young children.

Back to the Past: Roots of Mathematical Thinking

comments from mathematicians

You know those people you sometimes meet, the ones who earn their bread as computer programmers and then go home at nights and cool down by doing mathematical brainteasers? How did they get that way? Where did their zest for things mathematical come from? After all, if we understood something about that, we might be able to make mathematics as contagious as measles.

Most mathematicians leave a trail of theorems rather than auto-biographies. But if you poke around in the lore that surrounds them, you do come across some thought-provoking bits here and there:

• Jean Piaget, the famous Swiss developmental psychologist, was fond of a childhood memory he had heard from an anonymous mathematician friend of his. This friend recalls sitting in his garden looking at a ring of stones. He counted them first in one direction and then in the opposite direction. He remembers being stunned at the discovery that the total was always the same, no matter what the order.

• In the 1700's, Karl Friedrich Gauss was a rambunctious school-boy. (Later he was to become an astronomer with many discoveries about the moon to his credit.) One day he and his classmates were punished by being told to add up all the numbers from one to a hundred. Only moments later, Gauss was up at the teacher's desk with 5050 written on his slate. When the astonished teacher asked him how he got the total, young Gauss explained that between 0 and 100 there are 50 pairs of numbers each adding up to a 100 (99 + 1, 98 + 2, etc.) and then the single 50 that is left.

• Norbert Weiner, a well-known twentieth century mathematician, swears he could never learn his multiplication tables. Instead, he discovered all kinds of numerical patterns that permitted him to remember what other people just sit down and memorize (for instance, that the products of nine's table always add up to nine with the last digit going down by one each time: 9, 18, 27, 36).

If you turn to people you can interview, you can find out even more. Here is Joseph Walters, a senior scientist at TERC in Cambridge, Massachusetts, who does research and development of math and science technology education:

I think that families specialize; you know, there are word families, or families where everyone is a musician. In a way, my family was a number family. I have a theory you can tell what a family is into by finding out how they spend time on a long car trip. What I remember doing on car trips was what we called the **doubling game**.

There is this mathematical fact . . . , if you double the thickness of a piece of paper 40 times, it will reach all the way to the moon. Now that's not so easy to believe. So when we'd get tired of watching out the window, we'd start this heated discussion: "How many pieces of paper in an inch?" "So how thick is one piece of paper?" "So double it; now double that. . . ." It always came out the same — by the thirty-eighth time it would be as thick as the distance to the moon. I suppose I got kind of addicted to that kind of problem with all those steps and multi-

plications. I can remember my best friend and I staying in at recess. We'd wipe the whole blackboard clean, start way over in the corner, and figure out how many inches in a light year. When the bell rang, and the kids started pouring back in, there we'd be with this giant number stretching across the board.

Mark Palmer is an architect and engineer who works at the National Institute of Standards and Technology in Washington, DC:

I think I've always liked playing with what's beautiful and what works. I grew up in this house in San Francisco that was built right into the side of a steep hill. As a little kid, I remember thinking that when I was in the basement I was also deep inside the hill.

The garden in back went practically straight up. There was an ugly concrete retaining wall holding back the hill. My father wanted to put a mosaic on it; everyone thought he was crazy. For several years we collected stones wherever we went. He spent weeks, maybe months, working out the physics. My sort-of grandmother drew the design. Every weekend we were out there laying in a new panel.

Upstairs, there were amazing small things; I especially remember a porcelain statue of Hamlet. He had very long thin fingers. He was delicate, breakable, but left out in the open where you could stare at those fingers and wonder how they were made.

Erin Phelps works at the Murray Research Center at Radcliffe College where she coordinates statistical analyses of large data sets:

When I was growing up I had no brothers — I was the oldest of three girls. I think I was the outlet for my father, who was a chemical engineer. I remember for instance that one Christmas when I was in school he gave me a really good metal slide rule.

In school I did well at math, but I just thought I was an all-around student. When it came time for senior high, I wanted to go on in math; but my parents pushed me towards the arts and social sciences. They thought that's where girls belonged. When it came time for college, I was on my own. My family didn't think that girls needed college, but I was determined. By working I kept myself in college, and it was a good thing I did. It was there that I discovered I had a real aptitude for math.

Looking back makes me think how important it is that **all** *children get a chance to do a great deal in many different kinds of math. Anyone who shows interest or skill — boy or girl — should be encouraged to pursue it as hard as he or she can. Without belief, encouragement, and opportunity, children will never develop strong math skills; and children with unsuspected math abilities, like girls, will never discover their aptitude.*

What sense can be made of such snatches of memory? They may not add up to a foolproof recipe for making mathematicians, but even such snapshots contain clues. Apparently, there are all kinds of mathematical thinkers: some who thrill to rules, others who adore giant numerals, and still others for whom mathematics is a tool for making beautiful things. But whichever flavor of mathematician you're after, you need more than rulers, sharp pencils, and tough instruction. In addition, you need:

- curiosity about underlying rules and patterns;
- time enough to investigate those patterns;
- courage to try solutions that lie off the beaten path;
- energy to pursue solutions;
- other human beings who show you what pleasure there is in understanding how the world works;
- a willingness to catch a severe case of that same pleasure.

Math Milestones: Abilities in Children of Different Ages

by Suzanne McWhorter Colvin

For some, mathematics is nothing more than a subject in school that has no relationship to the outside world. It is seen as a process of applying a set of rules to a set of numbers to get a set of answers (Wearne & Hiebert). But for young children, mathematics could be something very different. It could be a chance to organize and make sense of what must seem at times to be an incomprehensible world. It could allow children to see what relationships are present in their environment and how elements of their environment are connected.

What was a huge mass of *stuff* can, with the assistance of ordering, matching, counting, and sizing up, become red stuff, blue stuff, tall stuff, stuff you wear, stuff used for eating, a lot of stuff, or just a little stuff! With such skills, the world around the child gradually begins to make sense and become more manageable. For this reason, good mathematics is something both welcomed and enjoyed by young children.

Mathematics Takes Many Shapes

Say *mathematics* or *arithmetic* and most people see pages of numerals to be matched to groups of hats, a number line, or addition problems. But, in fact, the world of math is enormous, even when it is tailored to what interests children. Leaving aside the counting series and the calculations involved in adding, subtracting, multiplying, or dividing, mathematics also includes:

Classifying. The kind of order-making activity involved in sorting beads from blocks, or red beads from blue ones. It also involves some intriguing, and not so easy to solve, questions like: "Is a clam an animal?" Or, "Do dragons go with dinosaurs?"

Comparing. Here is where operations like "He has more dominoes than me!" come into play. Even children engage in more abstract sorts of comparisons: "Her bike turn is longer than mine was." Or, "Is snow heavier than rain?"

Ordering. This kind of activity involves placing items, or even ideas, in a sequence. The sequence can run from tiny to enormous, from feather-weight to heavy, from longest hair to shortest hair, from earliest born to last born.

Patterning. When children make patterns, they create special kinds of orders in which they play with ideas of arrangement, balance, repetition, and symmetry. Just as older children discover that every tenth digit ends in zero, younger children may paint patterns of red and yellow stripes, build a block rocket with two equal fins on either side, or dig a series of bigger and bigger holes in the sand.

Measuring. Measuring involves all kinds of decisions about how much or how long. Two five year olds can solve their debate about who's tallest by measuring back to back. Children can crowd onto the carpets in a room to see which one holds more. Someone can measure a clay corral to see if she has made it big enough for her clay horse (all she has to do is hold the horse up to it).

Shape and space. Children explore shapes in doing puzzles, in painting forms, or in deciding if they found an apple or a banana inside their lunch bag. Children encounter basic

aspects of space whenever they use or think about boundaries, arrangements, or positions: squinching down to crawl through a pipe, recreating a table setting in a playhouse, trying to draw the difference between a pigeon and an owl.

Mathematics Comes Through Many Channels

Children need to learn mathematics in many ways. If children are faced with a steady diet of conventional number symbols, whether they are words, pictures, or numerals, they are being offered far too few channels. In fact, there is considerable research which shows that unless children understand the underlying mathe-

matical concepts, they can't really grasp the way that such symbols work (Kamii).

Children need many forms of learning to build up such concepts, including:

Perception. Early on (and perhaps throughout our lives) we experience at least some mathematical information directly: through what we see, hear, and touch. Before teachers ask that children acquire words or number terms to describe concepts of *more*, *less*, or *equal*, it is essential that children know these ideas in an eyes-on and hands-on way. Can a child hold two squares and just by feeling them tell which is bigger and which is smaller? Can a child hear two car

Photograph by Judy Burr

horns and figure out which one is closer?

Concrete problem solving. Before children understand about quarts and pints, the only real way to understand whether the contents of one jar will fit in another is to tilt and pour. Before they understand about measuring with feet and inches, children can tell if they have enough rope for jumping by trying it out. Children share out the apple slices by each taking one, then two, and so on. These concrete and very motivating encounters provide a foundation for later work with notions of volume, measurement, and division.

Invented representations. While numerals are still too hard to make and too abstract, children can use their early diagramming and drawing abilities to represent their mathematical procedures and the results of their work. Tally marks can record how many blocks in a tower, pictures will show where the taller books go, simple maps of the classroom can capture the fact that the blocks are close to the water table; but the plants are far, far away.

Numerals and counting. For children old enough to understand the way numbers work, every day is full of occasions when they can practice and extend their understanding: numbering the pages in a handmade book, reading the outdoor thermometer, figuring out how many children are present and absent.

Mathematics Comes in Stages

No level or type of mathematics springs full blown into a four year old's head. Young children are limited in the kinds of mathematical experiences they can understand at any given age (Driscoll). An infant can recognize her mother as tall and her brother as small. A baby will go right for the several shiny buttons on

the floor, ignoring the blocks. But that kind of selective attention is a long way from the five year old's sorting and categorizing skills. It is important, therefore, that we offer concepts and skills in a sequence that respects what children of different ages (or stages of development) can order, sort, add, or understand.

Although space won't permit looking at every age child and every area of mathematics, it is worthwhile to consider how children at different ages (or levels of development) might be encouraged to engage in the full range of mathematics.

• Late Infancy: 12-18 Months

Infants' mathematical knowledge comes from direct action, sensory exploration, and face-to-face interaction, not from hearing adults count or label two bunnies or three dogs. As a consequence, a varied physical environment is any baby's best math textbook.

Shape and space. Give babies shapes they can and can't get into such as doorways, boxes, and tunnels. See that they meet up with space where they will and won't fit. Play outdoors with them in a vigorous way so that they know in their arms and legs what it means to be higher than, above, outside, inside. Don't stand still, let them watch you go up and down, disappear, and reappear.

As they play, talk out loud about what they are doing so that they can learn the words that will help them communicate about shapes and spaces. Use your voice dramatically: Shout "You are WWAAYY UUUPPPP!" and whisper "Lizzie is hiding inside the tunnel."

When you buy toys, actively think about purchasing items that will highlight shape and space: buy red balls from basketball size down to golf ball

size. Display materials to show off differences (or similarities) in size and shape.

Comparing. Infants understand opposites and drastic contrasts best. Best of all, they like processes like dumping and filling, standing up and knocking down, present and absent (that's what's so charming to them about peek-a-boo). Impromptu games that play on these kinds of changes give them great pleasure.

Similarly, games of too big and too small work well: Make a row of shoes from an infant's bootie to a giant man's slipper and try them all on. (A great toddler joke is a teacher with a baby sock on her big toe or another toddler flopping across the floor in shoes that look as big as barges.)

Patterns and classifying. At this age, pattern making can be as simple as knowing the pattern of where things go or adding more to a giant line of blocks that stretches across the classroom. Even very young children can think about matching: they can recognize Peter's blanket and carry it to him, they can find the other parts of the big wooden train.

Problem solving. Infants are forever problem solving: they are trying to reach faraway objects, cram one inside another, squeeze into spaces not exactly made for small bodies. What they need is an environment which promotes their problem solving in artful ways. Imagine a playhouse with openings of various sizes and heights, rather than the all-too-usual door and windows.

Through experiment, infants will discover which gaps they can make it through and which openings are good for dropping their supplies through. Think about several doll beds and several dolls. The jamming and cramming that will go on is really a lesson in size relations.

• Three Year Olds

Compared to infants, three year olds have three (hmmmm . . .) novel resources for learning: 1) a new level of fine motor development, 2) a new set of social skills, and 3) language to talk over what's on their minds. At the same time, they have learned something about standards and rules. They can be embarrassed by not knowing an answer or how to negotiate an activity. Consequently, it is important to establish a classroom atmosphere which encourages explorations, without shaming children for false starts or lack of understanding.

Shape and space. Three year olds can certainly learn the names for all kinds of shapes and spaces. But more than acquiring labels, they need to think about the concepts the words stand for. For instance, three year olds can begin to think about the consequences of shapes. Talk with them about the fact that round things will roll and square ones won't. Then bring out a cylinder and talk about how it can roll and stand still. Given their eye-hand control, they paint, draw, and model clay. They will enjoy *reading* the shapes they make by chance and trying to make new ones. Get them to wonder, too: "How come a tall skinny clay shape droops and a thick one stays upright?" "It's funny, isn't it, that little pictures can be of big things." (Ever seen an elephant in a book?)

Comparing. The social awareness of three year olds makes a wonderful setting for thinking about same and different: who has on the same, similar, or different shirts; who has drunk the same amount of milk; who has the same amount of clay? (This is an interesting question since it comes in pancakes, globs, and sausage shapes.)

Raise good questions: "When Camilla gives you a block, what happens to her pile?" Three year olds aren't nearly as wedded to the present moment as younger children, so their comparisons can include remembered and imagined things. "How big were you when you were a baby, how big will you be when you are 8, when you are 42?"

Patterns and classifying. Threes can be engaged in pattern making and classifying in social ways: passing out items, one for everybody; everyone taking a partner, only two kids on each tire swing. Because of their memories, imaginations, and language abilities, they can begin to talk about larger patterns they observe: what happens when sand dries, how high is the snow on the window today (and what might have made it go up or down), are there getting to be more or fewer leaves outside, do bigger leaves always come from bigger trees?

Problem solving. The complex social world of three year olds faces them with plenty of problems to solve: three trikes and two kids, six orange sections and four children. Less than absolute rules, children need strategies for approaching and solving these everyday math problems. It is never too soon to use discussion: "What do you think we should do with the leftover oranges, Sasha? What about you, Erik?" Letting threes work with older children also provides them with an enlarged store of possibilities.

• Five Year Olds

Compared to three year olds, fives are remarkable for their interest in systems — whether those systems are Legos for building or a rapid fire line of questioning about "What happens after you count to 999,999?" They have a level of persistence and attention that makes them want to watch a

cocoon over several weeks or keep track of whose building has the most blocks. Moreover, they are fluent, not just in spoken language, but in construction and drawing, as well. In fact, they are quite prepared to take on the task of recording and reflecting on their own mathematical ideas (even if they don't use *real* writing and numbers to do it). Let them make books to keep track of the fattest, the longest, the tallest items they make from blocks, Legos, Construx. Give them rolls of calculator paper (spread horizontally) and let them experiment with writing the biggest (e.g., longest) number they can.

Shape and space. In a way, five year olds are ripe for a more probing kind of experimenting with shapes and spaces. If they fill a series of containers with wet sand, they can dump out the contents in a row and try to judge which held more. Where disagreements persist, set them to figuring out how to solve them — how can they use water (or beans) to do it? Using their building books, take them for a walk outside and let them pick out buildings with the same sorts of shapes.

Patterns and classifying. Children of this age can begin to think about much more complicated kinds of patterns or groupings. Some of them can sort along two dimensions, making collections of small and pointy, large and pointy, small and round, and large and round leaves. They can make handsome paintings in which they play with color and shape alternations. Moreover, many fives are old enough to enjoy the fuzziness involved in much of pattern making and categorization: If you are sorting red and blue beads, where does a red bead with blue stripes go? Where does a blue bead with red stripes go? Some children may even be able to think about the meaning behind simple kinds of representational patterns. Graph the time of the sun going down

Photograph by Bonnie Neugebauer

children draw in a picture of themselves at eight.

A Checklist for Preschool Mathematics Development

As a way of rounding out this look at the steps in children's mathematical development, here is a chart of abilities preschool children can develop by the age of five. It contains the many types of skills mentioned earlier. It can be used to plan math curricula or to keep track of individual children's mathematical development. Use it to spark ideas, but keep in mind that it is designed as a starting place. A full curriculum or a thorough assessment of a child requires more than a checklist.

References

Driscoll, M. J. "Research Within Reach: Mathematics in Kindergarten," **The National Institute of Education Publication**, November 1979.

Kamii, C. **Number in Preschool and Kindergarten**. Washington, DC: NAEYC, 1982.

Wearne, D., and J. Hiebert. "Teach for Thinking in Mathematics," **Childhood Education**, March/April 1984.

between August and November, study and talk about the pattern of points. What do children think will happen in the coming weeks?

Problem solving. Five year olds still often solve problems by trial and error, but they are teetering on the edge of being able to predict what will happen. Activities can draw out this ability: Ask children to choose a pitcher large enough to hold juice for 24 children; talk about what would happen if they chose one too small or too large. Draw outlines of an infant, a toddler, and a five year old; have

Suzanne McWhorter Colvin was a graduate student in early childhood education with a special interest in young children's mathematical development at the University of Florida in Gainesville.

Mathematical Concepts for Early Childhood

Classifying: Sorting or forming groups by similar attributes

Discovering concepts of likenesses and differences
Sorting by one attribute (sorting by shape, for example)
Discovering other similarities and regrouping accordingly (sort by color then by shape)
Classifying on the basis of negation (squares and non-squares)

Terms: Sets, groups, sort, alike, different, words describing shapes, colors, sizes, textures

Comparing: Establishing a relationship between objects

Comparing amounts or sizes (amounts of milk in glasses, heights, etc.)
Comparing numbers of things (determining which set has more)
Comparing sets requiring one-to-one correspondence (one black chip for one red chip)

Terms: More than, greater than, less than, shorter, longer, fewer, least, heavier, equal, same

Ordering: Arranging in a sequence

Ordering by size (long to short, thin to fat, large to small)
Ordering by number (most to least, least to most)
Ordering by time (first to last, morning, afternoon, night)

Terms: First, second, third, longer, shorter, fewer, fewest, order, sequence, row, line, stack, next, then, later

Patterning: A form of ordering containing an element of repetition, should move from simple to complex

Becoming aware of patterns (recognizing that the stripes of a shirt are in a pattern)
Describing patterns (telling what the pattern looks like)
Extending patterns (changing a red, green, red, green pattern to red, green, blue . . .)
Completing patterns (asking a child to finish a pattern already started — red, blue, red . . .)
Repeating patterns (given a pattern, reproduce or repeat it)
Creating patterns (making up a pattern)

Terms: Patterns, alike, different, over and over, repeat, design

Measuring: Deciding how long or how much — length, weight, volume

Continuous measurement with direct comparisons (placing objects side by side)
Continuous measurement with indirect comparisons (using a stick or string to compare lengths)

Terms: Longer, shorter, heavier, more, less, little, big, long, higher, larger

Shape and space: Space refers to boundaries, arrangements, and positions; shape refers to form

Positions (over, under, above, below, between)
Distance (near, far, close)
Construction (making and changing space, fitting into a space)
Topological space experiences (altering shapes while retaining properties of being open or closed)
Euclidean shape experiences (squares, triangles, and other rigid shapes)

Numbers:

Experiencing cardinal numbers (how many)
Experiencing ordinal numbers (first, second, etc.)
Experiencing numbers that label (Room 10)

Terms: One, two, three, first, second, how many

Counting:

Counting by rote (reciting the names of the numerals in order)
Counting rationally (attaching a numeral name to a series of objects)

Terms: One, two, three, etc.

Numerals: Symbols for numbers which should be introduced following an understanding of the cardinality of a set (children can identify and understand how many are in a set)

Organizing, representing, and recording mathematical information: Drawing, using language to describe, building models, creating simple graphs with real objects

Problem solving: Relating mathematics to the real world and including the following —

Real objects
Action or manipulation
Interest and challenge
A realization on the part of the child that he has the ability to solve the problem

Preserving the Sanctity of Childhood: Numeracy, Morality, and the High-Tech Bullies

by Keith Jefferson

There are two things which seem very far removed from one another: arithmetic and moral principles . . . nevertheless the child who has a right introduction to arithmetic will have a quite different feeling of moral responsibility in later life than the child who has not.

— Rudolf Steiner, Oxford, 1922

The late Gregory Bateson, biologist husband of the late anthropologist Margaret Mead, was fond of reminding his listeners that if we "break the pattern which connects the items of learning we necessarily destroy all quality." Surely our goal in education is to preserve this connecting pattern; and yet as we lurch towards the twenty-first century, education seems to be only able to present the most bewildering of pictures as to what this pattern aims to connect. Art and science? Humankind and nature? Graduates and the work force? Head, heart, and hands?

With few exceptions, to matriculate through the American educational system, from the preschool/kindergarten age on up to high school, is to experience a kind of socio-spiritual dismemberment that mocks any real sense of wholeness or symbiotic totality in life. Parents are repeatedly told that education is aimed at the body, mind, and spirit — a three-membered entity that through education emerged as an interdependent whole. But is this *interdependent wholeness* what parents are seeing in their children? More importantly, does the current process and method of education in our schools mirror this integration of elements? Or are we, as Bateson suggests, in danger of *breaking a pattern that connects*; this time the pattern that connects the child with himself and ultimately with the world.

Somewhere along the line towards our future, we have missed out on a basic attitude with our children — a humanizing attitude that undercuts the pressure that parents, educators, and children no doubt feel from modern life. In our heart of hearts we know that the acquisition of information alone is a shallow and inadequate basis for education. Education of our young people must somehow not only reflect intelligence, but permeate itself with that force that illuminates the ultimate aim of human intelligence.

An abiding sense of morality, of the greatest and highest good towards which our awakened sensibilities and skills can be addressed, must become an integral part of how we teach children. Bateson, Steiner, and many others have constantly warned that for each step we take in our technological advancement, twice as many steps must be taken to further that which safeguards our highest human ethics and values and ultimately gives meaning to the adage "as in heaven, also on earth."

Who or What Determines Computer Readiness?

Picture for a moment the child between the age of three and seven. Now juxtapose that picture with one of a bank of computers. It seems a shame to try to get a wiggly, pudgy-fingered four year old behind the keyboard of a personal computer — especially in light of the survey from MIT which finds no significant advantage in having a child interact with a computer — especially the kindergarten/preschool age child. There is no doubt that a comprehensive liter-

acy level of an adolescent should include a modicum of computer competency — but when is it realistic to begin?

This question is at the center of the whole hotly debated computer-in-the-schools controversy. It is unfortunate that much of the pro-computer thrust is predicated by largely unproven, unresearched notions that children will not find their place in the career world unless they begin computer classes IMMEDIATELY! Who really determines what the young child needs educationally? Teachers? Child psychologists? Parents? Computer marketers? Scientific magazines and journals? The fact is they all do — and all for vastly different reasons. The pattern that connects?

When one thinks of the bouncing, tumbling energy of this age group, it is difficult to understand why educators do not utilize this boundless energy and openness as an educational basis, instead of the early *molding* that so often characterizes our approach. Instead of taking the models of development our children are biologically bound to follow (i.e. metaphoric, symbolic language structures unfolding in the mid-brain from the ages of 4 to 7 as the basis of *operational* thinking at 11 or 12 years old), we are introducing *operational* thinking modes (computer skills and languages) before the child is ready for them. Even more chilling is the practice of utilizing motivational *tricks* to get our children to adapt to patterns which just do not match the biological stage of their developmental growth.

Number and Morality

Sharing, dividing, giving, adding, taking away — these elements of early math conceptualization can also be easily seen as seed forces, if you will, of a developing moral life. Coupled with the utilization of the young child's innate sense of wholeness, his

deep love of rhythm and rhyme, as well as his buoyant, boundless physical energy (a clear, untampered picture of the nature of the human will in its primal form), an introduction to math, with this picture of the child in mind, takes on a richer, more whole-child-engaging form than could be derived from even the most colorful of computers. Steiner, in his above-mentioned quote from an address to a group of British Waldorf school teachers and educators in Oxford, goes on:

When a child has acquired the habit of adding things together we get a disposition which tends to be desirous and craving. In proceeding from the whole to its parts (for example, 6 is 2 x 3, rather than 2 x 3 is 6), the child has less tendency to acquisitiveness and rather tends to develop what could be called in a Platonic sense, in the highest sense, considerateness and moderation . . . one's moral likes and dislikes are intimately bound up with the manner in which one has learned to deal with number.

Those who would scoff at the concept of morality and number, the idea that a child may enter into the world of moral character and the magical realm of number through the same door and at the same time, only underlines the sad fact that in these times education is looked upon as a science rather than an art — the child as *programmable software* upon which our programs can be tested and curricula as a warehouse of *data* to be fed to the child as a kind of kiddie prerequisite to career planning. Simply stated, we need to be aware of the sanctity of childhood, especially early childhood, and utilize a little moral muscle and common sense to keep *high-tech bullies* from intimidating the true playground of the young child.

Keith Jefferson is a former principal of the Waldorf School in Santa Barbara, California. He is currently a consultant for Waldorf in the Marin County area of California.

Insights on Mathematical Learning

collected by Regina Brown

Sylvia Ashton-Warner

"Ferns make wonderful counting boards. When we were on long trips when our children were little, we would sometimes give them a big frond to count, and as an occupational toy I can recommend it. Costs nothing. Just pick one from the side of the road. And all the time they were learning fundamental things about natural form.

Clover is an incomparable activity in threes and it's just out the door. Also it is something you can pick in quantities and bring inside. For upper primers learning to count in threes and for the Little Ones learning to count to three. But counting the impermanent birds is the most concentrated game, involving a self-imposed quiet and watchful eyes, and there's the drawing or painting or clay record to follow.

The last time we went we each took a small branch and counted the leaves on it. They ranged from six to seventeen. Then I told the children to count a hundred trees in the willow plantation, touching each tree, and afterwards we went on down to the sand by the river and wrote our numbers with sticks." Sylvia Ashton-Warner, **Teacher** (New York: Bantam Books, Inc., 1963), pp. 68-69.

Maria Montessori

"In dealing with normal children, we must *await* this spontaneous investigation of the surroundings, or, as I like to call it, this *voluntary explosion* of the exploring spirit. In such cases, the children experience a joy at each *fresh discovery*. They are conscious of a sense of dignity and satisfaction which encourages them to seek for new sensations from their environment and to make themselves spontaneous *observers*. . . ." Maria Montessori, **The Montessori Method** (New York: Schocken Books, 1964), pp. 227, 228.

"The greatest triumph of our educational method should always be this: *to bring about the spontaneous progress of the child*."

Mary Baratta-Lorton

"A page of abstract symbols, no matter how carefully designed or simplified, *because of its very nature*, cannot involve the child's senses the way real materials can. Symbols are not *the concept*, they are only a representation of the concept, and as such are abstractions describing something which is not visible to the child. Real materials, on the other hand, can be manipulated to illustrate the concept concretely, and can be experienced visually by the child." Mary Baratta-Lorton, **Mathematics Their Way** (Menlo Park, CA: Addison-Wesley Publishing Company, 1976), p. xiv.

"When children give wrong answers, it is not so often that they are wrong as that they are answering another question. The job is to find out what question they are, in fact, answering." David Page in Baratta-Lorton, Vol. XI, p. 13.

Jean Piaget

"The construction of whole numbers occurs in the child in close connection

with the construction of seriations and class inclusions. One must not think that a young child understands numbers simply because he can count verbally. In his mind numerical evaluation is for a long time linked with the spatial arrangement of the elements. . . . Naturally, there can be no question of operatory numbers before the existence of a conservation of numerical groups independent of spatial arrangement." Jean Piaget and Barbel Inhelder, **The Psychology of the Child** (New York: Basic Books, Inc., 1969), p. 104.

Herbert Ginsburg and Sylvia Opper

"A good school should encourage the child's activity, and his manipulation and exploration of objects. When the teacher tries to bypass this process by imparting knowledge in a verbal manner, the result is often superficial learning. But by promoting activity in the classroom, the teacher can exploit the child's potential for learning, and permit him to evolve an understanding of the world around him." Herbert Ginsburg and Sylvia Opper, **Piaget's Theory of Intellectual Development, An Introduction** (Englewood Cliffs, NJ: Prentice-Hall, Inc., 1969), p. 221.

"First the child physically sorts or otherwise manipulates objects. He feels various forms and in this way, among others, perceives the differences among them. He may put different forms in different places. Later, he can sort the objects solely on a mental level. He does not need to separate things physically, but he can do it mentally. Later still, he can perform inclusion operations on the (imagined) classes of objects. He can consider that a hypothetical class includes and is 'larger than' its constituent sub-class. Thus, knowledge of classification does not merely involve facts, but actions as well: physical sorting, mental sorting, men-

Photograph by Francis Wardle

tal inclusion operations. Furthermore, most of these actions are non-verbal." Ginsburg and Opper, p. 222.

"Interest and learning are facilitated if the experience presented to the child bears some relevance to what he already knows but at the same time is

sufficiently novel to present incongruities and conflicts." Ginsburg and Opper, p. 223.

Glenn Doman

"Tiny children can actually see and

almost instantly identify the actual number of objects as *well* as the numeral *if they are given the opportunity to do so early enough in life and before they are introduced to numerals.*

This gives tiny children a staggering advantage over all adults in learning to do and actually to *understand* what is happening in arithmetic." Glenn Doman, **Teach Your Baby Math** (New York: Pocket Books, 1979), pp. 36-37.

"Tiny children *are* doing math better and more easily than adults. Hundreds of tiny children are presently doing math and doing it with true understanding of what is happening. Only a minute percentage of adults truly understand what actually happens in math." Doman, p. 65.

"The best time to teach your child to do math with little or no trouble is when he is about one or two years old. Beyond two years of age, the teaching of math gets harder every year. If you are willing to go to a little trouble, you can begin when your baby is 18 months old or — if you are very clever — as early as 8 months." Doman, p. 81.

Joe Nathan

"A group of five year olds were interviewed as they used their school's computers and the (Logo) program to create various patterns. They were asked if doing this was more fun than drawing flowers or walking through a field with flowers. 'God makes real flowers,' explained one youngster. 'These are only pretend. And the flowers in the field are prettier.' Several other children said they like to do different things at different times. 'Sometimes it's computer time, sometimes it's drawing time.' What's the most fun, they were asked. The five

year olds have a long list: 'Playing with my cat, playing with *He-man*, sleeping over at my friend's house, watching TV.' 'Doing something with my parents — that's the best,' says a little boy. Several of the others agree quickly, 'Yes, it's always more fun to do something with my parents.' One youngster, who clearly would rather be working with the computer than talking to an adult, responds: 'Playing with a computer is more fun than drawing or walking. The computer makes me feel like I'm God.'" Joe Nathan, **Micro-Myths: Exploring the Limits of Learning with Computers** (Minneapolis, MN: Winston Press, Inc., 1985), pp. 15-16.

Herbert Leff

"What traits or characteristics could a shark's jaws be used to measure? How about talkativeness or bigmouthedness, for instance? ('Jovial Jack jumps from two to six shark jaws after the first round of drinks.') Hunger would certainly seem a possibility, as would meanness. ('When I'm over three shark jaws hungry, I'm at least eight shark jaws mean!') Or you might use shark jaws to measure holes in someone's logic, the bitingness of pieces of gossip, or the degree to which prices *rip you off*. Take a few minutes and see how many other things you can potentially evaluate in terms of shark jaws. In each case, how does using this unusual unit of measure lead you to feel about what you are evaluating?" Herbert L. Leff, **Playful Perception: Choosing How to Experience Your World** (Burlington, VT: Waterfront Books, Inc., 1984), p. 70.

Galileo

"That vast book which stands forever open before our eyes, the universe,

cannot be read until we have learned the language and become familiar with the characters in which it is written. It is written in mathematical language, without which means it is humanly impossible to comprehend a single world." Galileo

Arnold Chance

"I venture to suggest that if one were to ask for a single attribute of the human intellect which would most clearly indicate the degree of civilization of a race, the answer would be the power . . . of reasoning, and that this power could best be determined in a general way by the mathematical skill which members of the race displayed." Arnold Chance, writing about the Rhind Mathematical Papyrus, a translation of an ancient Egyptian document (named after the man who gave it to the British Museum)

G. H. Hardy

"A mathematician, like a painter or a poet, is a maker of patterns." G. H. Hardy

A Third Grader

"Patterns are when things take turns." A third grader

Regina Brown was the director of Latchkey at University Place in Tacoma, Washington, and a student in the Department of Scientific and Technical Communications at the University of Washington in Seattle.

Help's at Hand!
Resources for Math Activities

by Karen Stephens

Young children should experience math every day through spontaneous as well as teacher planned math activities. Did the last part of that statement make your stomach tighten? Does the thought of coming up with a math activity for tomorrow trigger panic in your otherwise confident "teacher-self"? When saying your program has a "well-rounded curriculum," do you sheepishly hope no one asks specifically about your *math* curriculum? Relax, you're not alone! Some of the most highly educated people have an inferiority complex when it comes to math! But, never fear, there is help right around the corner — at your local bookstore or library.

Compiled in this article is a variety of teacher resources to help you become more confident in planning math activities. In fact, if you take time to investigate the resources, you may even become *eager* to include math in your daily curriculum (no, I am not kidding!). When reviewing the books, you are bound to realize you know more about early childhood math than you thought.

Math is more than workbooks, fractions, and multiplication tables. It is all about hands-on involvement, the "stuff" of sensory childhood delights: collecting shells, sorting beans, patterning blocks, pouring water from one container to another, making molds in sand, and rolling balls of clay. These are the types of activities you will find in this resource listing — and not a ditto sheet among them!

In this article, you'll also find math resources for children. Listed is a bevy of the old, cherished standby — the picture book. Picture books about numbers have evolved beyond mere "counting books."

Authors and illustrators have created works of art to introduce children to sophisticated math concepts such as shape, pattern, size, design, measurement, and time.

There's yet another avenue for children's math explorations within your reach: math computer games. Don't balk at the idea! I have been amazed when witnessing children's attention span, eye-hand coordination, and conceptual knowledge develop through computer play. Computers are an everyday feature of children's primary education. The role computers can play in early childhood education should not be overlooked. In fact, early childhood is an ideal time to introduce computers to the classroom. What better way to prevent children from developing computer phobias so prevalent among "pre-1970's babies." Computer math games are all about processing and applying information. Same educational processes, simply a new learning tool! Luckily for you, there is a growing selection of developmentally appropriate math computer games from which to select.

In recent years, as in the past, many early childhood teachers, children's authors and illustrators, and now computer program developers, have put their writing talents to work to lend you their expertise on teaching math. So, as you can see, when it comes to planning math activities, help really is at hand! And it's all within your reach.

Books with Math Activities for Young Children

Baratta-Lorton, Mary. **Mathematics Their Way**. Menlo Park, CA: Addison-Wesley Publishing Company, 1976.

A planned mathematics curriculum used by many elementary schools — packed with ideas for questions, activities, and concept building.

Baratta-Lorton, Mary. **Workjobs II** (photographs by John Madden and Geri Madden). Menlo Park, CA: Addison-Wesley Publishing Company, 1979.

Twenty teacher-made activities which teach and reinforce concept of numbers. Discussion includes rationale of activity (all are carefully thought through), construction of materials, assessment of child's current understanding, and descriptions of child use at various levels of learning.

Brown, Sam Ed. **One, Two, Buckle My Shoe** (illustrated by Jula Libonn). Beltsville, MD: Gryphon House, 1982.

Ideas for activities and teacher-made materials which promote mathematical learning. Simple format.

Charlesworth, Rosalind, and Deanna J. Radeloff. **Experiences in Math for Young Children** (2nd Edition). New York: Delmar, 1978.

Basic, practical ideas for teaching children the processes of math. Includes information on how children learn math.

Chenfeld, Mimi Brodsky. **Creative Activities for Young Children**. San Diego, CA: Harcourt Brace Jovanovich, 1983.

One chapter each on shapes and numbers. Integrates topic into talk times, art, music, movement, and field trips.

Church, Ellen Booth, and Karen Miller. **Learning Through Play: Blocks**. New York: Scholastic, 1990.

Hands-on activities for 2-5 year olds. Numerous activities to stimulate mathematical concept development. Other curriculum areas addressed as well.

Croft, Doreen J. **An Activities Handbook for Teachers of Young Children** (5th Edition). Boston: Houghton Mifflin Co., 1990.

Book includes one chapter each for math and cooking. Math chapter includes developing a math learning center. Activities relate to classification — sorting and comparing, conservation, seriation and measurement — and equivalence — matching and pairing, number concepts, and ordinal numbers.

Faggella, Kathy. **Concept Cookery**. Bridgeport, CT: First Teacher Press, 1985.

Book integrates cooking activities within specific themes. The shapes, math, and opposite sections will be most helpful to those planning math activities.

Faggella, Kathy, and Martha A. Hayes. **Counting on Math**. Bridgeport, CT: First Teacher Press, 1988.

Basic activities for 4-6 year olds. The following areas are addressed: All About Me; Language Development; Seasons; Science and Cooking; Colors; Children's Literature; Community Helpers; and Celebrations.

Gilbert, Anne Green. **Teaching the Three Rs Through Movement Experiences**, 1977. Burgess Publishing Company, 7108 Ohms Lane, Minneapolis, MN 55435.

Using one's whole body to solve problems and explore ideas can be great fun. Math (also language arts, social studies, science, and art) becomes a physical, imaginative, intellectual experience — body math!

Granovetter, Randy, and Jeanne James. **Sift & Shout: Sand Play Activities for Children Ages 1-6**. Lewisville, NC: Kaplan Press, 1989.

Fun sand activities arranged by age. Many address math concepts such as shape and measuring volume.

Honig, Alice S. **Playtime Learning Games for Young Children**. Syracuse, NY: Syracuse University Press, 1982.

Many of these games include mathematical concepts as the goal or within the context of the game. Because these activities are for toddlers, this resource provides ideas for very early mathematical learning.

James, Jeanne C., and Randy F. Granovetter. **Waterworks: A New Body of Waterplay Activities for Children Ages 1-6**. Lewisville, NC: Kaplan Press, 1987.

Activities arranged by age. The activities section for 5 and 6 year olds includes the most math.

Johnson, Barbara. **Cup Cooking** (illustrated by Betty Plemons). Lake Alfred, FL: Early Educators Press, 1978. Distributed by Gryphon House, 10726 Tucker Street, Beltsville, MD, (800) 638-0928.

Recipes for child preparation of individual portions promote involvement and firsthand discoveries. Cup Cooking Starter Kit also available. Set includes single step charts on 5 1/2 x 11 1/2 cards (4 recipes, 22 cards).

Kamii, Constance. **Number in Preschool and Kindergarten: Educational Implications of Piaget's Theory**. Washington, DC: National Association for the Education of Young Children, 1982.

*Discusses alternatives to teacher math through drill and worksheets. Empha-*sizes ways children learn math through typical early childhood program activities.

Keyser, Tamara J., and Randall J. Souviney. **Measurement and the Child's Environment**. Santa Monica, CA: Goodyear Publishing, 1980.

Hands-on measurement activities — early childhood through grade 6.

Kohl, Mary Ann, and Cindy Gainer. **MathArts**. Beltsville, MD: Gryphon House, 1996.

Creative art projects introduce young children to early math concepts.

Kranyik, Margery. **A Year of Shapes**. Bridgeport, CT: First Teacher Press, 1990.

Basic activities for 4-6 year olds. Organized as follows: Shapes in My World — Fall Shapes; Winter Shapes; Spring Shapes; and Summer Shapes.

Miller, Karen. **The Outside Play and Learning Book**. Beltsville, MD: Gryphon House, 1989.

Sections on water play, sand play, and woodworking are rich with math opportunities!

Moomaw, Sally, and Brenda Hieronymous. **More Than Counting: Whole-Math Activities for Preschool and Kindergarten**. Minneapolis, MN: Redleaf Press, 1995.

Hands-on math activities integrated throughout the curriculum, includes grid games, path games, graphing, gross motor play.

Richardson, Katy. **Developing Number Concepts Using Unifix Cubes**. Menlo Park, CA: Addison-Wesley Publishing Company, 1984.

*An extensive, informative resource on using Unifix cubes to teach mathemat-*ical concepts. Although written for elementary teachers, the guidelines can help early childhood teachers enrich children's experiences with these materials.

Richardson, Lloyd I., Kathy L. Goodman, Nancy N. Hartman, and Henri C. LePique. **A Mathematics Activity Curriculum for Early Childhood and Special Education**. New York: Macmillan Publishing Co., 1980.

Provides developmental activities up to age eight. Strong emphasis on understanding Piaget's stages of conceptual development.

Skeen, Patsy, Anita Payne Garner, and Sally Cartwright. **Woodworking for Young Children**, 1984. NAEYC, 1834 Connecticut Avenue NW, Washington, DC 20009-5786, (800) 424-2460.

Rationale and objectives for providing woodworking experiences for young children. Fine, detailed discussion of tool selection. Guidelines for setting up the center as well as the situation. Excellent basic resource.

Stephens, Karen. **Block Adventures: Build Creativity and Concepts Through Block Play**. Bridgeport, CT: First Teacher Press, 1991.

Hands-on activities to highlight math skills through block building. Also includes dramatic play, science, and art.

Stone, Janet. **Hands-On Math**. New York: HarperCollins, 1989.

Hands-on math activities for 3-6 year olds.

Thompson, David. **Easy Woodstuff for Kids** (illustrated by Stacy Buhler). Beltsville, MD: Gryphon House, 1981.

Simple woodworking projects for young children with basic skills. List and rationale for tool selection is valuable. Well illustrated.

Veitch, Beverly, and Thelma Harmes. **Cook and Learn. Pictorial Single Portion Recipes. A Child's Cookbook**. Menlo Park, CA: Addison-Wesley, 1981.

Easy-to-follow recipes that are easy to reproduce for classroom use. Nice variety of recipes including multicultural.

Warren, Jean. **1 2 3 Math: Pre-Math Activities for Working With Young Children**. Everett, WA: Warren Publishing House, Inc., 1992.

Activities for basic math processes such as counting, sorting, grouping, matching, measuring, etc. Sections on recognition of shapes and numbers, developing thinking skills, and understanding relationships are included. Activities can be incorporated into daily routines. Easy-to-follow format.

Waite-Stupiansky, Sandra, and Nicholas G. Stupiansky. **Learning Through Play: Math**. New York: Scholastic, 1992.

Hands-on math activities for 2-5 year olds. Emphasizes the basic math processes.

Explore Math Through Children's Books

Counting Books

Abby Aldrich Rockefeller Folk Art Center. **The Folk Art Counting Book**. New York: Harry N. Abrams, Inc., 1992.

Aker, Suzanne. **What Comes in 2s, 3s, & 4s**. New York: Simon & Schuster, 1990.

Aliki. **The Two of Them**. New York: Greenwillow, 1979.

Anno, Masaichiro and Mitsumasa. **Anno's Mysterious Multiplying Jar**. New York: Philomel Books, 1983.

Anno, Mitsumasa. **Anno's Counting Book**. New York: Thomas Y. Crowell, 1975.

Anno, Mitsumasa. **Anno's Counting House**. New York: Putnam, 1982.

Aylesworth, Jim. **One Crow: A Counting Rhyme Book**. New York: Harper & Row, Publishers, 1988.

Baker, Keith. **Big Fat Hen**. New York: Harcourt Brace & Co., 1994.

Bang, Molly. **Ten, Nine, Eight**. New York: Greenwillow Books, 1983.

Bawden, Juliet, and Helen Pask. **1 One-Year-Old: Counting Children 1 to 10**. New York: Henry Holt & Co., 1989.

Beeson, Bob. **Ten Little Circus Mice**. Nashville, TN: Ideals Publishing Corp., 1993.

Blumenthal, Nancy. **Count-A-Saurus**. New York: Four Winds Press, 1989.

Bond, Michael. **Paddington's 1, 2, 3**. New York: Pufflin Books, 1990.

Bowen, Betsy. **Gathering: A Northwoods Counting Book**. New York: Little Brown & Co., 1995.

Brett, Jan. **The Twelve Days of Christmas**. New York: Dodd, Mead and Co., 1986.

Brown, Marc. **Hand Rhymes**. New York: E. P. Dutton, 1985.

Burgess, Mark. **One Little Teddy Bear**. New York: Viking, 1991.

Carter, David A. (illustrator). **Over in the Meadow: An Old Counting Rhyme**. New York: Scholastic, 1992.

Cherrill, Paul. **Ten Tiny Turtles: A Crazy Counting Book**. New York: Ticknor & Fields, 1995.

Clements, Andrew. **Mother Earth's Counting Book**. Natich, MA: Picture Book Studio, 1992.

Crews, Donald. **Ten Black Dots**. New York: Greenwillow Books, 1986.

Davies, Charlotte (editor). **My First Look at Counting**. New York: Random House, 1991.

Dunbar, Joyce. **Ten Little Mice**. New York: Harcourt Brace Jovanovich, Publishers, 1990.

Dunham, Meredith. **Numbers: How Do You Say It? English, French, Spanish, Italian**. New York: Lothrop, Lee & Shepard Books, 1987. *(Multicultural)*

Enderle, Judith Ross, and Stephanie Gordon Tessler. **Six Creepy Sheep**. New York: Puffin Books, 1992. *(Halloween book)*

Ernst, Lisa Campbell. **Up to Ten and Down Again**. New York: Lothrop, Lee & Shepard Books, 1986.

Falwell, Cathryn. **Feast for 10**. New York: Clarion Books, 1993. *(Multicultural)*

Feelings, Muriel. **Moja Means One**. New York: The Dial Press, 1971. *(Multicultural)*

Fleming, Denise. **Count!** New York: Henry Holt & Co., 1992.

Geddes, Anne. **1, 2, 3**. San Rafael, CA: Cedco Publishing, 1995.

Giganti, Jr., Paul. **Each Orange Had 8 Slices**. New York: Greenwillow Books, 1992.

Giganti, Jr., Paul. **How Many Snails?** New York: Greenwillow Books, 1988.

Greenfield, Eloise. **Aaron and Gayla's Counting Book**. New York: Writers & Readers, 1993.

Grossman, Virginia, and Sylvia Long. **Ten Little Rabbits**. San Francisco: Chronicle Books, 1991.

Hague, Kathleen. **Numbears**. New York: Scholastic, 1986.

Harshman, Marc. **Only One**. New York: Dutton, 1993.

Heinst, Marie. **My First Number Book**. New York: Dorling Kindersley Limited, 1992.

Herman, Gail. **Count the Days of Hanukkah**. New York: Scholastic, 1993.

Hindley, Judy. **One by One**. Cambridge, MA: Candlewick Press, 1996.

Hoban, Tana. **Count and See**. New York: Macmillan Publishing Co., 1972.

Hoban, Tana. **26 Letters and 99 Cents**. New York: Greenwillow Books, 1987.

Hooker, Yvonne. **One Green Frog**. New York: Grosset & Dunlap, 1981.

Hughes, Shirley. **When We Went to the Park**. New York: Lothrop, Lee & Shepard Books, 1985.

Hulme, Joy. **Sea Squares**. New York: Hyperion Books for Children, 1991.

Hutchins, Pat. **The Doorbell Rang**. New York: Greenwillow Books, 1986.

Hutchins, Pat. **1 Hunter**. New York: Greenwillow Books, 1982.

Jackson, Woody. **Counting Cows**. New York: Harcourt Brace & Co., 1995.

Kawai'ae'a, Keiki Chang. **Let's Learn to Count in Hawaiian**. Aiea, HI: Island Heritage Publishing, 1988, (808) 487-7299. (Multicultural)

Kessler, Ethel and Leonard. **Two, Four, Six, Eight**. New York: Dodd, Mead and Co., 1980.

Kindersley, Dorling. **Lifesize Animal Counting Book**. New York: Dorling Kindersley Limited, 1992.

Kitamura, Satashi. **When Sheep Cannot Sleep: The Counting Book**. New York: Farrar Straus Giroux, 1986.

Linden, Ann Marie, and Lynne Russell. **One Smiling Grandma: A Caribbean Counting Book**. New York: Dial Books for Young Readers, 1992. (Multicultural)

MacDonald, Suse, and Bill Oakes. **Numblers**. New York: Dial Books for Young Readers, 1988.

McGrath, Barbara Barbieri. **The M&M's Counting Book**. Watertown, MA: Charlesbridge Publishing, 1994.

McMillan, Bruce. **Counting Wildflowers**. New York: Lothrop, Lee & Shepard Books, 1986.

McMillan, Bruce. **Eating Fractions**. New York: Scholastic, 1991.

Marzollo, Jean. **Ten Cats Have Hats: A Counting Book**. New York: Scholastic, 1994.

Merriam, Eve. **12 Ways to Get to 11**. New York: Simon & Schuster, 1993.

Micklethwait, Lucy. **I Spy Two Eyes**. New York: William Morrow & Co., 1993.

Morozumi, Atsuko. **One Gorilla**. New York: Farrar, Straus & Giroux, 1990.

Murphy, Chuck. **My First Book of Counting**. New York: Scholastic, 1991.

Owen, Annie. **Annie's One to Ten**. New York: Alfred A. Knopf, 1988.

Owens, Mary Beth. **Counting Cranes**. Boston: Little, Brown & Co., 1993.

Pallota, Jerry. **The Icky Bug Counting Book**. Watertown, MA: Charlesbridge Publishing, 1992.

Peek, Merle. **Roll Over: A Counting Song**. Boston: Houghton Mifflin, 1981.

Pinkney, Andrea Davis. **Seven Candles for Kwanza**. New York: Dial Books for Young Readers, 1993. (Multicultural)

Powers, Christine. **My Day With Numbers**. New York: Scholastic, 1992.

Pragoff, Fiona. **How Many? From Zero to Twenty**. New York: Doubleday, 1987.

Princzes, Elinor J. **One Hundred Hungry Ants**. Boston: Houghton Mifflin, 1993.

Reidy, Hannah. **Crazy Creatures Counting**. New York: De Agostini Editions, Ltd., 1996.

Schade, Susan, and Jon Buller. **The Noisy Counting Book**. New York: Random House, 1987.

Sheppard, Jeff. **The Right Number of Eggplants**. New York: Harper & Row, Publishers, 1990.

Sloat, Teri. **From One to One Hundred**. New York: Dutton Children's Books, 1991.

Tafuri, Nancy. **Who's Counting?** New York: Greenwillow Books, 1986.

Thompson, Susan L. **One More Thing, Dad**. Chicago: Albert

Whitman & Co., 1980. *(Nice portrayal of an involved dad in a non-sexist role)*

Thornhill, Jan. **The Wildlife 1 2 3**. New York: Simon & Schuster, 1989.

Trinca, Rod, and Kerry Argent. **One Woolly Wombat: An Australian Counting Book**. New York: Kane/Miller Book Publishers, 1985. *(Multicultural)*

Tudor, Tasha. **1 is One**. New York: Checkerboard Press, a division of Macmillan Publishing Co., 1956.

Unstead, Sue (editorial director). **My First Look at Numbers**. New York: Random House, 1990.

Van Fleet, Matthew. **One Yellow Lion**. New York: Penguin Books, 1992.

Wallace, Karen. **Why Count Sheep? A Bedtime Book**. New York: Hyperion Books, 1993.

Walsh, Ellen Stoll. **Mouse Count**. New York: Harcourt Brace Jovanovich Publishers, 1991.

Walton, Rick. **How Many How Many How Many**. Cambridge, MA: Candlewick, 1993.

Wedgman, William. **One, Two, Three**. New York: Hyperion Books, 1995.

Wildsmith, Brian. **Brian Wildsmith's 1, 2, 3s**. New York: Franklin Watts, 1965.

Yektai, Niki. **Bears at the Beach: Counting 10 to 20**. Brookfield, CT: Millbrook Press, 1996.

Yoshi. **One, Two, Three**. Natich, MA: Picture Book Studio, 1991.

Ziefert, Harriet. **How Many Eggs?** New York: Harper-Collins, 1991.

Books About Shape

Anno, Mitsumasa. **Anno's Journey**. New York: Putnam, 1979.

Anno, Mitsumasa. **In Shadowland**. New York: Orchard Books, 1988.

Bowen, Betsy. **Tracks in the Wild**. Boston: Little, Brown & Co., 1993.

Budney, Blossom. **A Kiss is Round**. New York: Lothrop, Lee & Shepard Books, 1969.

Burns, Marilyn. **The Greedy Triangle**. New York: Scholastic, 1995.

Carle, Eric. **My Very First Book of Shapes**. New York: Crowell, 1974.

Dorros, Arthur. **Animal Tracks**. New York: Scholastic, 1991.

Dunbar, Fiona. **You'll Never Guess!** New York: Dial, 1991. *(Guessing shadow shapes)*

Ehlert, Lois. **Circus**. New York: HarperCollins, 1992.

Ehlert, Lois. **Color Farm**. New York: Lippincott, 1990.

Ehlert, Lois. **Color Zoo**. New York: Lippincott, 1989.

Farber, Norma. **Return of the Shadows**. New York: HarperCollins, 1992.

Fleischman, Paul. **Shadow Play**. New York: Harper & Row, Publishers, 1990.

Grifalconi, A. **The Village of Round and Square Houses**. New York: Norton, 1987. *(Multicultural)*

Hoban, Tana. **I Read Signs**. New York: Greenwillow Books, 1983.

Hoban, Tana. **I Read Symbols**. New York: Greenwillow Books, 1983.

Hoban, Tana. **Round and Round and Round**. New York: Greenwillow Books, 1983.

Hoban, Tana. **Shadows and Reflections**. New York: Greenwillow Books, 1990.

Hoban, Tana. **Shapes and Things**. New York: Macmillan Publishing Co., 1986.

Hoban, Tana. **Shapes, Shapes, Shapes**. New York: Greenwillow Books, 1979.

Hutchins, Pat. **Changes, Changes**. New York: Macmillan Publishing Co., 1971.

Murphy, Chuck. **My First Book of Shapes**. New York: Scholastic, 1992.

Rogers, Paul. **The Shape Game**. New York: Henry Holt & Co., 1989.

Schwager, Istar. **Shapes**. Lincolnwood, IL: Publications International, 1992.

Seuss, Dr. **The Shape of Me and Other Stuff**. New York: Random House, 1973.

Shaw, Charles G. **It Looked Like Spilt Milk**. New York: Harper & Row, Publishers, 1947.

Skofield, James. **Round and Around**. New York: Harper & Row, Publishers, 1993.

Stevenson, Robert Louis. **Block City**. New York: E. P. Dutton, 1988.

Unstead, Sue (editorial director). **My First Look at Shapes**. New York: Random House, 1990.

Wegman, William. **Triangle, Square, Circle**. New York: Hyperion Books, 1995.

Books About Size

Allen, Pamela. **Who Sank the Boat?** New York: Coward-McCann, 1985.

Arnold, Tim. **The Three Billy Goats Gruff**. New York: Maxwell Macmillan International, 1993.

Asch, Frank. **Little Fish, Big Fish**. New York: Scholastic, 1992.

Beck, Ian. **Five Little Ducks**. New York: Henry Holt & Co., 1992.

Bennett, Jill. **Teeny Tiny**. New York: G. P. Putnam's Sons, 1986.

Beskow, Elsa. **The Tale of the Little, Little Old Woman**. Edinburgh, Scotland: Floris Publishing, 1989.

Brett, Jan. **Goldilocks and the Three Bears**. New York: Dodd, Mead & Co., 1987.

Brett, Jan. **The Mitten**. New York: G. P. Putnam's Sons, 1989.

Bright, Robert. **My Red Umbrella**. New York: William Morrow and Company, 1959.

Carle, Eric. **The Tiny Seed**. Natich, MA: Picture Book Studio, 1987.

DePaola, Tomie. **Jamie O'Rourke and the Big Potato: An Irish Folktale**. New York: G. P. Putnam's Sons, 1992.

Galdone, Paul. **The Three Billy Goats Gruff**. New York: Clarion Books, 1973.

Hoban, Tana. **Big Ones, Little Ones**. New York: Greenwillow Books, 1976.

Hoban, Tana. **One Little Kitten**. New York: Scholastic, 1979.

Koopmans, Loek (illustrator). **Any Room for Me?** (retelling of **The Mitten**). Edinburgh, Scotland: Floris Publishing, 1992.

Lord, John Vernon. **The Giant Jam Sandwich**. Boston: Houghton Mifflin, 1972.

Lyon, David. **The Biggest Truck**. New York: Lothrop, Lee & Shepard Books, 1988.

Porter, Sue. **Little Wolf and the Giant**. New York: Simon & Schuster, 1989. *(Great surprise ending! Moral of the story — don't stereotype people based on size.)*

Silverman, Erica. **Big Pumpkin**. New York: Macmillan Publishing Co., 1992. *(Halloween book)*

Srivastava, Jane Jonas. **Spaces, Shapes and Sizes**. New York: Thomas Y. Crowell, 1980.

Zolotow, Charlotte. **Big Sister and Little Sister**. New York: Harper & Row, Publishers, 1966.

Stories with Numbers in Them

Akins, Susan. **Number Nine Duckling**. Honesdale, PA: Boyds Mills Press, 1993.

Brett, Jan. **Comet's Nine Lives**. New York: G. P. Putnam's Sons, 1996.

Brown, Margaret Wise. **Four Fur Feet**. New York: Hyperion, 1994.

Carle, Eric. **Rooster's Off to See the World**. Natick, MA: Picture Book Studio, 1972.

Carle, Eric. **The Very Hungry Caterpillar**. New York: Philomel Book, 1969.

Cauley, Lorinda Bryan. **Three Blind Mice**. New York: G. P. Putnam's Sons, 1991.

Chalmers, Mary. **Six Dogs, Twenty-Three Cats, Forty-Five Mice, and One Hundred Sixteen Spiders**. New York: Harper & Row, Publishers, 1986.

Croll, Carolyn. **The Three Brothers: A German Folktale**. New York: G. P. Putnam's Sons, 1991. *(Multicultural)*

Cutler, Daniel Solomon. **One Hundred Monkeys**. New York: Simon & Schuster, 1991.

Eco, Umberto, and Eugenio Carmi. **The Three Astronauts**. New York: Harcourt Brace Jovanovich, Publishers, 1989. *(Multicultural)*

Ets, Marie Hall, and Aurora Labastida. **Nine Days to Christmas. A Story of Mexico**. New York: Viking Press, 1959. *(Multicultural)*

Gag, Wanda. **Millions of Cats**. New York: Coward, McCann & Geoghegan, 1956.

Galdone, Paul. **Three Little Kittens**. New York: Clarion Books, 1986.

Hooper, Meredith. **Seven Eggs**. New York: Harper & Row, Publishers, 1985.

Jones, Carol. **This Old Man**. New York: Houghton-Mifflin, 1990.

Martin, Jr., Bill, and John Archambault. **Knots on a Counting Rope**. New York: Henry Holt & Co., 1987. *(Multicultural and special needs)*

Seuss, Dr. (Theodor S. Geisel). **The 500 Hats of Bartholomew Cubbins**. New York: Random House, 1938.

Viorst, Judith. **The Tenth Good Thing About Barney**. New York: Atheneum, 1983.

Young, Ed. **Seven Blind Mice**. New York: Philomel Books, 1992.

Zolotow, Charlotte. **One Step, Two. . . .** New York: Lothrop, Lee & Shepard Books, 1981.

Books About Time or the Passage of Time

Anastasio, Dina. **It's About Time** New York: Grosset & Dunlap, 1993.

Aylesworth, Jim. **The Completed Hickory Dickory Dock**. New York: Atheneum, 1990.

Brown, Margaret Wise. **Goodnight Moon**. New York: HarperCollins, 1947.

Bruchac, Joseph, and Jonathon London. **American Year of Moons**. New York: Philomel Books, 1992.

Bruchac, Joseph, and Jonathon London. **Thirteen Moons on Turtle's Back: A Native**. New York: Philomel Books, 1991.

Bunting, Eve. **How Many Days to America? A Thanksgiving Story**. New York: Clarion Books, 1990. (*Multicultural*)

Carle, Eric. **The Grouchy Ladybug**. New York: Thomas Y. Crowell, 1977.

Edmonds, William. **Reader's Digest Kids Big Book of Time**. Marshall Editions Developments Ltd., 1994.

Florian, Douglas. **A Year in the Country**. New York: Greenwillow Books, 1989.

Fox, Mem. **Time for Bed**. New York: Harcourt Brace & Co., 1993.

Franklin, Kristine L. **The Old, Old Man and the Very Little Boy**. New York: Atheneum, 1992. (*Multicultural*)

Gibbons, Gail. **The Seasons of Arnold's Apple Tree**. New York: Harcourt Brace Jovanovich, 1984.

Isn't It Time? Cambridge, MA: Candlewick Press, 1996.

Kindersley, Dorling. **My First Look at Time**. New York: Random House, 1991.

Lesser, Carolyn. **The Goodnight Circle**. New York: Harcourt Brace & Co., 1984.

McMillan, Bruce. **Step by Step**. New York: Lothrop, Lee & Shepard Books, 1987.

McPhail, David. **Farm Boy's Year**. New York: Atheneum, 1992.

Murphy, Jill. **Five Minutes' Peace**. New York: G. P. Putnam's Sons, 1986.

Pearson, Susan. **How Many Days to My Birthday?** New York: Lothrop, 1992.

Roberts, Bethany. **Two O'Clock Secret**. Chicago: Albert Whitman & Company, 1992.

Rockwell, Anne. **First Comes Spring**. New York: Thomas Y. Crowell, 1985.

Russo, Marisabina. **Only Six More Days**. New York: Greenwillow Books, 1988.

Russo, Marisabina. **Waiting for Hannah**. New York: Greenwillow Books, 1989.

Viorst, Judith. **Sunday Morning**. New York: Macmillan Publishing Co., 1993.

Books About Sorting, Grouping, Seriation, Patterning, or Comparing

Brown, Ruth. **If At First You Do Not See**. New York: Holt, Rinehart and Winston, 1982.

Browne, Philippa-Alys. **A Gaggle of Geese: The Collective Names of the Animal Kingdom**. New York: Simon & Schuster, 1996.

Crews, Donald. **Bicycle Race**. New York: Greenwillow Book, 1985.

Gillham, Bill. **What Happens Next?** New York: G. P. Putnam's Sons, 1985.

Heller, Ruth. **A Cache of Jewels and Other Collective Nouns**. New York: Grosset & Dunlap, 1987.

Hoban, Tana. **Dots, Spots, Speckles, and Stripes**. New York: Greenwillow Books, 1987.

Hoban, Tana. **Is It Red? Is It Yellow? Is It Blue?** New York: Greenwillow Books, 1978. (*Explores color, shapes, sizes, and relationships*)

Hoban, Tana. **More Than One**. New York: Greenwillow Books, 1981.

Hoban, Tana. **Spirals, Curves, Fan-shapes and Lines**. New York: Greenwillow Books, 1992.

Hong, Lily Toy. **Two of Everything**. New York: Albert Whitman & Company, 1992.

McMillan, Bruce. **One, Two, One Pair**. New York: Scholastic, 1991.

Pluckrose, Henry. **Knowabout Pattern**. New York: Franklin Watts, 1988.

Pluckrose, Henry. **Knowabout Sorting**. New York: Franklin Watts, 1988.

Sawicki, Norma Jean. **Little Red House**. New York: Lothrop, Lee & Shepard Books, 1989. (*Seriation by size*)

Stein, Sara. **A Piece of Red Paper**. Princeton, NJ: Small World Enterprises, 1973.

Tompkins, Jasper. **The Catalog**. La Jolla, CA: The Green Tiger Press, 1981.

Books About Measurement

Adams, Pam. **Ten Beads Tall**. New York: Child's Play International, 1988.

Asch, Frank. **Short Train, Long Train**. New York: Scholastic, 1992.

Chwast, Seymour. **Tall City, Wide Country**. New York: The Viking Press, 1983.

Hoban, Tana. **Is It Larger? Is It Smaller?** New York: Greenwillow Books, 1985.

Lioni, Leo. **Inch by Inch**. New York: Astor Books, 1960.

Maestro, Betsy and Giulio. **Temperature and You**. New York: Lodestar Books, 1990.

Weiss, Monica. **How Many? How Much? Measuring**. New York: Troll Associates, 1992.

Books About Distance and Maps

Hartman, Gail. **As the Crow Flies**. New York: Bradbury Press, 1991.

Jenkins, Steve. **Looking Down**. New York: Houghton-Mifflin, 1995.

Lionni, Leo. **Inch by Inch**. New York: Scholastic, 1960.

Sweeney, Joan. **Me on the Map**. New York: Crown Publishers, 1996.

Math Game and Project Books for School-Agers

Adler, David. **Calculator Riddles**. New York: Holiday Houe, 1995.

Anno, Mitsumasa. **Anno's Math Games**. New York: Philomel Books, 1982.

Anno, Mitsumasa. **Anno's Math Games II**. New York: Philomel Books, 1982.

Anno, Mitsumasa. **Anno's Math Games III**. New York: Philomel Books, 1991.

Burns, Marilyn. **The I Hate Mathematics! Book**. Boston: Little, Brown & Co., 1975.

Burns, Marilyn. **Math for Smarty Pants**. Boston: Little, Brown & Co., 1982.

Clever Kids: Math Ages 5-7. Chicago, IL: World Book, 1995

Godrey, Neale S. **The Kids' Money Book**. New York: Checkerboard Press, 1991.

Grover, Max. **Amazing and Incredible Counting Stories: A Number of Tall Tales**. New York: Harcourt Brace, 1995.

Scieszka, Jon, and Lane Smith. **Math Curse**. New York: Viking, 1995.

Sports Math Mania! New York: Sports Illustrated Kids Books.

Wilkinson, Elizabeth. **Making Cents. Every Kid's Guide to Money: How to Make It, What to Do With It**. New York: Little, Brown & Co., 1989.

Resources to Help You Select Children's Math Computer Software

Buckleitner, Warren (editor). **Children's Software Revue**. Six issues per year. Children's Software Revue, 44 Main Street, Flemington, NJ 08822, (800) 993-9499.

A newsletter dealing with the latest trends in children's software. Will also do customized computer searches of children's software.

Hohman, Charles. **Young Children and Computers**. Ypsilanti, MI: The High/Scope Press, 1990.

Basic information on preschoolers working with computers. Includes one chapter on computers and children's logical/mathematical thinking and one chapter on computers at group times, work times, and circle times.

Salpeter, Judy. **Kids and Computers: A Parent's Guide**. Indianapolis, IN: Alpha Books, Prentice Hall Computer Publishing, 1991, (800) 428-5331.

Children's Software Revue's pick for best resource book on children and computers.

After five and a half cherished years as an early childhood teacher, Karen Stephens became director of Illinois State University Child Care Center, an NAEYC accredited program. The center is a lab school for college child development students. Ms. Stephens is also an instructor for the Family and Consumer Sciences Department at ISU, Normal, Illinois.

Countdown to a Climate for Early Mathematical Learning

Here is an informal checklist for the qualities of an environment that fosters strong mathematical learning in young children. Read the questions, observe your class yourself; then work with other teachers, your director, even an interested parent to figure out where you're strong and where you'd like to make changes.

Do you understand children's early mathematical development?

- Do you have a strong feel for what children of different ages are interested in finding out about mathematics?

- Do you know how to translate your knowledge into activities that are within children's range, but which stretch their thinking?

- Do you (and other teachers) know what you want children to know about mathematics by the time they move on to another classroom or school?

Do you offer children many ways to go about thinking mathematically?

- Do you have strategies for using children's bodily sensations to learn about quantities?
  . . . What about offering an infant a very big and a small ball?
  . . . Could you ask a three year old to pick a small and big square out of a bag?
  . . . Have you ever gone walking with five year olds and asked them to pick out sounds of things that are near and far away?

- Can you use classroom conversation and discussion to help children find powerful and appropriate ways to express their observations and questions?

- Do you use a range of other forms to communicate mathematical ideas?
  . . . Gestures (pinch vs. arms wide gesture)
  . . . Block models (house vs. castle, whole city)
  . . . Drawing
  . . . Notations (tallies for game scores, graphs, maps, etc.)

Is it a classroom where many kinds of mathematics are explored?

- Pattern making
- Comparing
- Problem solving
- Classifying
- Ordering
- Measuring
- Understanding shapes and spaces

Is the classroom "rich" in materials that can promote mathematical thinking?

- A water table with many sized containers
- Blocks, Legos, or Construx
- String, rope, sticks for measuring and comparing sizes
- Magnifying glasses for playing with sizes
- Bins, tubs, bowls for filling and emptying
- Compartmentalized trays along with good junk for sorting
- Books with language rich in size, shape, and amount language

Are you making good use of the teaching partners available to you?

- Can you set up a situation in which children learn from their peers?
- Do you ever use older children to work with younger ones?
- Have you involved parents? (There's a great "do it at home" sheet that begins on page 30 which can get you started.)

Is there an atmosphere of investigation?

- Do you have strategies to draw out a child's thinking?
    - . . . Can you pose good questions?
    - . . . Can you set up a discussion among children?
    - . . . Can you suggest experiments for them to test their ideas?
    - . . . Do you put out intriguing displays? Can you create a feeling of investment and curiosity?
    - . . . Do you ever wonder aloud?

. . . Do you leave projects up long enough so that children can really get a feeling for observing, recording, questioning?

. . . Do you get excited when children discover different bits and pieces of mathematics?

Is it a comfortable place to explore mathematical ideas?

- Is it a room where it's possible to learn from mistakes?
  . . . Do you ever talk about mistakes you make and what you learn?
  . . . Can you respond to spilled juice with a comment or question, rather than a command or reprimand?

- Is it a room where there's tolerance for different approaches?
  . . . Among teachers?
  . . . Among children?

- Are children free to use numbers in a range of ways?
  . . . Playfully ("My doll is twenty-two sixteens old.")
  . . . Descriptively ("I'm a ten, I'm big.")
  . . . To map out their level of understanding ("One, two, three . . . a lot.")
  . . . Practically (He has three crackers, and you said only two.")

Do you have time to observe individual children working on math?

- At the beginning, middle, and end of the year?
- Do you have ways of recording changes?
- Do you share these observations with parents?
- Do you ever give children a look at how they've changed?
- Do you have a master teacher, supervisor, or clinician you can turn to if you are concerned about a child?

Do you, as an adult, ever take time to refresh your curiosity about math?

- Do you play with the children's materials?
- Do you ever go to a science and technology museum?
- Do you try your hand at mathematical games and puzzles?

Discover the importance of wonder.

And teach it well.

This magnificent book provides thought-provoking information and practical, down-to-earth ideas you can use to help young children discover and explore the magic of the world that surrounds us.

In *The Wonder of It*, you'll find a wealth of information about the excitement of science and the importance of wonder in the lives of young children. Best of all, you'll find easy-to-implement, hands-on activities designed to support the curiosity of children, stimulate their thinking, help them ask good questions, and share their joy in discovery.

It's all right here in *The Wonder of It* for only $16. Order your copy by calling us at (800) 221-2864. Discover the importance of wonder. And teach it well.

Child Care Information Exchange
PO Box 2890 • Redmond, Washington 98073-2890